Know MY Heart

A Color-and-Pray DEVOTIONAL

SUSAN JONES

Good Books

New York, New York

Good Books books may be purchased in bulk at special discounts for sales promotion, corporate gifts, fund-raising, or educational purposes. Special editions can also be created to specifications. For details, contact the Special Sales Department, Good Books, 307 West 36th Street, 11th Floor, New York, NY 10018 or info@skyhorsepublishing.com.

Good Books is an imprint of Skyhorse Publishing, Inc.®, a Delaware corporation.

Visit our website at www.goodbooks.com.

10 9 8 7 6 5 4 3 2 1

Library of Congress Cataloging-in-Publication Data is available on file.

Cover illustration used under license from Shutterstock.com.

Print ISBN: 978-1-68099-283-0
Ebook ISBN: 978-1-68099-291-5

Printed in China

How to Use This Journal

This unique, 365-page color-and-pray journal provides you with a fun and creative way to add depth to your daily devotions. As you color each beautiful illustration, reflect on what God is telling you through the scriptures. Write a prayer for someone you love, or list the many gifts that God has bestowed upon you. *Know My Heart* will guide you on a colorful, year-long journey of devotion that leads you closer to God. As you open your heart to fill the lines of this journal, you'll discover more about yourself and your faith than you ever thought possible. Turn the page and begin adding your personal touch!

Date: _____

My Bible verse of the day:

_____
_____
_____
_____
_____
_____
_____

*What this verse means
in my life today:*

_____
_____
_____
_____
_____
_____
_____
_____
_____

My prayer to God:

_____
_____
_____
_____
_____
_____
_____
_____
_____
_____

Date: _____

Deep in my heart I feel:

_____
_____
_____
_____
_____
_____
_____
_____

I thank God for:

_____
_____
_____
_____
_____
_____
_____
_____
_____
_____

Today I can serve God by:

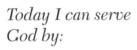

_____
_____
_____
_____
_____
_____
_____
_____
_____
_____

Date: _____

My Bible verse of the day:

_____

_____

_____

_____

_____

_____

What this verse means
in my life today:

_____

_____

_____

_____

_____

_____

_____

_____

_____

_____

My prayer to God:

_____

_____

_____

_____

_____

_____

_____

_____

_____

Date: _____

Today my heart is full of:

_____
_____
_____
_____
_____
_____

I hear God reminding me:

_____
_____
_____
_____
_____
_____
_____
_____

I believe God is teaching me:

_____
_____
_____
_____
_____
_____
_____
_____
_____
_____
_____
_____
_____
_____

Date: _____

My Bible verse of the day:

_____
_____
_____
_____
_____

*What this verse means in
my life today:*

_____
_____
_____
_____
_____
_____
_____
_____
_____

My prayer to God:

_____
_____
_____
_____
_____
_____
_____
_____
_____

Date: _____

Today I feel blessed because:

_____
_____
_____
_____
_____
_____
_____

I feel God in my heart when I:

_____
_____
_____
_____
_____
_____
_____
_____
_____

I have faith that God will:

_____
_____
_____
_____
_____
_____
_____
_____
_____
_____
_____
_____
_____

Date: _____

My Bible verse of the day:

_____
_____
_____
_____
_____
_____

*What this verse means in
my life today:*

_____
_____
_____
_____
_____
_____
_____
_____
_____
_____

My prayer to God:

_____
_____
_____
_____
_____
_____
_____
_____
_____
_____

Date: _____

My Bible verse of the day:

_____
_____
_____
_____
_____
_____

What this verse means in my life today:

_____
_____
_____
_____
_____
_____
_____
_____
_____
_____

My prayer to God:

_____
_____
_____
_____
_____
_____
_____
_____
_____
_____
_____

Date: _____

Deep in my heart I feel:

_____
_____
_____
_____
_____
_____

I thank God for:

_____
_____
_____
_____

_____
_____
_____
_____
_____

Today I can serve God by:

_____
_____
_____
_____
_____
_____
_____
_____
_____
_____

Date: _____

My Bible verse of the day:

_____
_____
_____
_____
_____
_____

What this verse means in my life today:

_____
_____
_____
_____
_____
_____
_____
_____
_____
_____

My prayer to God:

_____
_____
_____
_____
_____
_____
_____
_____
_____
_____

Date: _____

Today my heart is full of:

_____
_____
_____
_____
_____

I hear God reminding me:

_____
_____
_____

_____
_____
_____
_____
_____
_____
_____

I believe God is teaching me:

_____
_____
_____
_____
_____
_____
_____
_____
_____
_____
_____
_____
_____

Date: _____

My Bible verse of the day:

_____
_____
_____
_____
_____
_____
_____

What this verse means in my life today:

_____
_____
_____
_____
_____
_____
_____
_____
_____

My prayer to God:

_____
_____
_____
_____
_____
_____
_____
_____
_____
_____
_____
_____
_____

Date: _____

Today I feel blessed because:

_____

_____

_____

_____

_____

_____

I feel God in my heart when I:

_____

_____

_____

_____

_____

_____

_____

_____

_____

_____

_____

I have faith that God will:

_____

_____

_____

_____

_____

_____

_____

_____

_____

_____

_____

Date: _____

My Bible verse of the day:

_____
_____
_____
_____
_____
_____
_____

What this verse means in my life today:

_____
_____
_____
_____
_____
_____
_____
_____
_____

My prayer to God:

_____
_____
_____
_____
_____
_____
_____
_____
_____
_____
_____

Date: _____

My Bible verse of the day:

_____
_____
_____
_____
_____
_____

*What this verse means in
my life today:*

_____
_____
_____
_____
_____
_____
_____
_____
_____
_____
_____

My prayer to God:

_____
_____
_____
_____
_____
_____
_____
_____
_____
_____

Date: _____

Deep in my heart I feel:

_____
_____
_____
_____
_____
_____

I thank God for:

_____
_____
_____
_____
_____
_____
_____
_____
_____

Today I can serve God by:

_____
_____
_____
_____
_____
_____
_____
_____
_____
_____
_____
_____

Date: _____

My Bible verse of the day:

_____
_____
_____
_____
_____
_____
_____

What this verse means in my life today:

_____
_____
_____
_____
_____
_____
_____
_____
_____
_____

My prayer to God:

_____
_____
_____
_____
_____
_____
_____
_____
_____
_____

Date: _____

Today my heart is full of:

_____
_____
_____
_____
_____
_____
_____

I hear God reminding me:

_____
_____
_____
_____
_____
_____
_____
_____
_____
_____

I believe God is teaching me:

_____
_____
_____
_____
_____
_____
_____
_____
_____

Date: _____

My Bible verse of the day:

_____
_____
_____
_____
_____
_____

What this verse means in my life today:

_____
_____
_____
_____
_____
_____
_____
_____
_____

My prayer to God:

_____
_____
_____
_____
_____
_____
_____
_____
_____

Date: _____

Today I feel blessed because:

_____
_____
_____
_____
_____
_____
_____

I feel God in my heart when I:

_____
_____
_____
_____
_____
_____
_____
_____
_____
_____

I have faith that God will:

        _____
        _____
        _____
        _____
        _____
        _____
        _____
        _____
        _____
        _____

Date: _____

My Bible verse of the day:

_____
_____
_____
_____
_____
_____

What this verse means in
my life today:

_____
_____

_____
_____
_____
_____
_____
_____
_____
_____

My prayer to God:

_____
_____
_____
_____
_____
_____
_____
_____
_____
_____
_____

Date: _____

My Bible verse of the day:

_____
_____
_____
_____
_____
_____
_____

What this verse means in my life today:

_____
_____
_____
_____
_____
_____
_____
_____
_____
_____

My prayer to God:

_____
_____
_____
_____
_____
_____
_____
_____
_____

Date: _____

Deep in my heart I feel:

_____
_____
_____
_____
_____
_____
_____

I thank God for:

_____
_____
_____
_____
_____
_____
_____
_____
_____
_____

Today I can serve God by:

_____
_____
_____
_____
_____
_____
_____
_____
_____
_____

Date: _____

My Bible verse of the day:

_____
_____
_____
_____
_____
_____

What this verse means in my life today:

_____
_____
_____
_____
_____
_____
_____
_____
_____
_____

My prayer to God:

_____
_____
_____
_____
_____
_____
_____
_____
_____
_____
_____

Date: _____

Today my heart is full of:

_____
_____
_____
_____
_____
_____
_____

I hear God reminding me:

_____
_____
_____
_____
_____
_____
_____
_____
_____
_____

I believe God is teaching me:

_____
_____
_____
_____
_____
_____
_____
_____
_____
_____

Date: _____

My Bible verse of the day:

_____

_____

_____

_____

_____

_____

_____

What this verse means in my life today:

_____

_____

_____

_____

_____

_____

_____

_____

_____

My prayer to God:

_____

_____

_____

_____

_____

_____

_____

_____

_____

_____

Date: _____

Today I feel blessed because:

_____
_____
_____
_____
_____
_____

I feel God in my heart when I:

_____
_____
_____
_____
_____
_____
_____
_____
_____
_____
_____

I have faith that God will:

_____
_____
_____
_____
_____
_____
_____
_____
_____
_____
_____
_____
_____

Date: _____

My Bible verse of the day:

_____
_____
_____
_____
_____
_____

What this verse means in my life today:

_____
_____
_____
_____
_____
_____
_____
_____
_____
_____
_____

My prayer to God:

_____
_____
_____
_____
_____
_____
_____
_____
_____
_____
_____
_____
_____

Date: _____

My Bible verse of the day:

_____
_____
_____
_____
_____

What this verse means in my life today:

_____
_____
_____
_____
_____
_____
_____
_____
_____
_____

My prayer to God:

_____
_____
_____
_____
_____
_____
_____
_____
_____
_____
_____

Date: _____

Deep in my heart I feel:

_____
_____
_____
_____
_____
_____

I thank God for:

_____
_____
_____
_____
_____
_____
_____
_____
_____

Today I can serve God by:

_____
_____
_____
_____
_____
_____
_____
_____
_____

Date: _____

My Bible verse of the day:

_____
_____
_____
_____
_____

*What this verse means in
my life today:*

_____
_____
_____
_____
_____
_____
_____
_____
_____
_____

My prayer to God:

_____
_____
_____
_____
_____
_____
_____
_____
_____
_____
_____

Date: _____

Today my heart is full of:

_____
_____
_____
_____
_____
_____

I hear God reminding me:

_____
_____
_____
_____
_____
_____
_____
_____
_____

I believe God is teaching me:

_____
_____
_____
_____
_____
_____
_____
_____
_____
_____
_____

Date: _____

My Bible verse of the day:

_____
_____
_____
_____
_____
_____

What this verse means in
my life today:

_____
_____
_____
_____
_____
_____
_____
_____
_____
_____
_____

My prayer to God:

_____
_____
_____
_____
_____
_____
_____
_____
_____
_____

Date: _____

Today I feel blessed because:

_____
_____
_____
_____
_____
_____

I feel God in my heart when I:

_____
_____
_____
_____
_____
_____
_____
_____
_____

I have faith that
God will:

_____
_____
_____
_____
_____
_____
_____
_____

Date: _____

My Bible verse of the day:
_____
_____
_____
_____
_____
_____

What this verse means in
my life today:
_____
_____
_____
_____
_____
_____
_____
_____
_____
_____

My prayer to God:
_____
_____
_____
_____
_____
_____
_____
_____
_____
_____

Date: _____

My Bible verse of the day:

_____
_____
_____
_____
_____
_____

What this verse means in my life today:

_____
_____
_____
_____
_____
_____
_____
_____
_____
_____

My prayer to God:

_____
_____
_____
_____
_____
_____
_____
_____
_____
_____
_____
_____

Date: _____

Deep in my heart I feel:

_____
_____
_____
_____
_____
_____
_____

I thank God for:

_____
_____
_____
_____
_____
_____
_____
_____
_____
_____

Today I can serve God by:

_____
_____
_____
_____
_____
_____
_____
_____
_____
_____

Date: _____

My Bible verse of the day:

_____
_____
_____
_____
_____
_____
_____
_____

What this verse means in my life today:

_____
_____
_____
_____
_____
_____
_____
_____
_____
_____

My prayer to God:

_____
_____
_____
_____
_____
_____
_____
_____
_____
_____

Date: _____

Today my heart is full of:

_____

_____

_____

_____

_____

I hear God reminding me:

_____

_____

_____

_____

_____

_____

_____

_____

_____

_____

I believe God is teaching me:

_____

_____

_____

_____

_____

_____

_____

_____

_____

_____

Date: _____

My Bible verse of the day:

_____
_____
_____
_____
_____
_____

What this verse means in my life today:

_____
_____
_____
_____
_____
_____
_____
_____
_____
_____

My prayer to God:

_____
_____
_____
_____
_____
_____
_____
_____
_____
_____
_____

Date: _____

Today I feel blessed because:

_____
_____
_____
_____
_____
_____

I feel God in my heart when I:

_____
_____
_____
_____

_____
_____
_____
_____
_____
_____

I have faith that God will:

_____
_____
_____
_____
_____
_____
_____
_____
_____
_____
_____

Date: _____

My Bible verse of the day:

_____
_____
_____
_____
_____
_____

What this verse means in my life today:

_____
_____
_____
_____
_____
_____
_____
_____
_____
_____

My prayer to God:

_____
_____
_____
_____
_____
_____
_____
_____
_____
_____

Date: _____

My Bible verse of the day:

_____
_____
_____
_____
_____
_____

*What this verse means in
my life today:*

_____
_____
_____

_____
_____
_____
_____
_____
_____
_____

My prayer to God:

_____
_____
_____
_____
_____
_____
_____
_____
_____

Date: _____

Deep in my heart I feel:

_____
_____
_____
_____
_____
_____

I thank God for:

_____
_____
_____
_____
_____
_____
_____
_____
_____
_____

Today I can serve God by:

_____
_____

_____
_____
_____
_____
_____
_____
_____
_____

Date: _____

My Bible verse of the day:

_____
_____
_____
_____
_____
_____

*What this verse means in
my life today:*

_____
_____
_____
_____
_____
_____
_____
_____
_____
_____
_____

My prayer to God:

_____
_____
_____
_____
_____
_____
_____
_____
_____
_____

Date: _____

Today my heart is full of:

_____
_____
_____
_____
_____
_____
_____

I hear God reminding me:

_____
_____
_____
_____
_____
_____
_____
_____
_____
_____
_____

I believe God is teaching me:

_____
_____
_____
_____
_____
_____
_____
_____
_____
_____
_____

Date: _____

My Bible verse of the day:

_____
_____
_____
_____
_____
_____

What this verse means in my life today:

_____
_____
_____
_____
_____
_____
_____
_____
_____
_____
_____

My prayer to God:

_____
_____
_____
_____
_____
_____
_____
_____
_____

Date: _____

Today I feel blessed because:

_____
_____
_____
_____
_____
_____
_____

I feel God in my heart when I:

_____
_____
_____
_____
_____
_____
_____
_____
_____
_____

I have faith that God will:

_____
_____
_____
_____
_____
_____
_____
_____
_____
_____
_____

Date: _____

My Bible verse of the day:

_____
_____
_____
_____
_____
_____

What this verse means in my life today:

_____
_____
_____
_____
_____
_____
_____
_____
_____
_____

My prayer to God:

_____
_____
_____
_____
_____
_____
_____
_____
_____
_____
_____
_____

Date: _____

My Bible verse of the day:

_____
_____
_____
_____
_____
_____

What this verse means in my life today:

_____
_____
_____
_____
_____
_____
_____
_____
_____
_____

My prayer to God:

_____
_____
_____
_____
_____
_____
_____
_____
_____
_____

Date: _____

Deep in my heart I feel:

_____
_____
_____
_____
_____
_____

I thank God for:

_____
_____
_____
_____
_____
_____
_____
_____
_____
_____

Today I can serve God by:

_____
_____
_____
_____
_____
_____
_____
_____
_____
_____

Date: _____

My Bible verse of the day:

_____
_____
_____
_____
_____
_____
_____

What this verse means in my life today:

_____
_____
_____
_____
_____
_____
_____
_____
_____
_____

My prayer to God:

_____
_____
_____
_____
_____
_____
_____
_____
_____
_____
_____
_____

Date: _____

Today my heart is full of:

_____
_____
_____
_____
_____
_____

I hear God reminding me:

_____
_____
_____
_____
_____
_____
_____
_____
_____
_____
_____

I believe God is teaching me:

_____
_____
_____
_____
_____
_____
_____
_____
_____
_____
_____
_____
_____

Date: _____

My Bible verse of the day:

_____

_____

_____

_____

_____

_____

What this verse means in my life today:

_____

_____

_____

_____

_____

_____

_____

_____

_____

_____

My prayer to God:

_____

_____

_____

_____

_____

_____

_____

_____

Date: _____

Today I feel blessed because:

_____
_____
_____
_____
_____

I feel God in my heart when I:

_____
_____

_____
_____
_____
_____
_____
_____
_____
_____

I have faith that God will:

_____
_____
_____
_____
_____
_____
_____
_____
_____
_____
_____

Date: _____

My Bible verse of the day:

_____
_____
_____
_____
_____
_____
_____

What this verse means in my life today:

_____
_____
_____
_____
_____
_____
_____
_____
_____

My prayer to God:

_____
_____
_____
_____
_____
_____
_____
_____
_____
_____
_____
_____

Date: _____

My Bible verse of the day:

_____
_____
_____
_____
_____
_____

*What this verse means in
my life today:*

_____
_____
_____
_____
_____
_____
_____
_____
_____
_____

My prayer to God:

_____
_____
_____
_____
_____
_____
_____
_____
_____
_____

Date: _____

Deep in my heart I feel:

_____
_____
_____
_____
_____
_____

I thank God for:

_____
_____
_____
_____
_____
_____
_____
_____
_____
_____

Today I can serve
God by:

_____
_____
_____
_____
_____
_____
_____
_____
_____
_____

Date: _____

My Bible verse of the day:

_____
_____
_____
_____
_____

Love

What this verse means in my life today:

_____
_____
_____
_____
_____
_____
_____
_____
_____
_____

My prayer to God:

_____
_____
_____
_____
_____
_____
_____
_____
_____
_____

Date: _____

Today my heart is full of:

_____
_____
_____
_____
_____
_____

I hear God reminding me:

_____
_____
_____
_____
_____
_____
_____
_____
_____

I believe God is teaching me:

_____
_____
_____
_____
_____
_____
_____
_____
_____
_____
_____
_____

Date: _____

My Bible verse of the day:

_____
_____
_____
_____
_____
_____

*What this verse means in
my life today:*

_____
_____
_____
_____
_____
_____
_____
_____
_____
_____
_____

My prayer to God:

_____
_____
_____
_____
_____
_____
_____
_____
_____
_____
_____

Date: _____

Today I feel blessed because:

_____
_____
_____
_____
_____
_____

I feel God in my heart when I:

_____
_____
_____
_____
_____
_____
_____
_____
_____

I have faith that
God will:

_____
_____
_____
_____
_____
_____
_____
_____

Date: _____

My Bible verse of the day:

_____
_____
_____
_____
_____
_____

What this verse means in my life today:

_____
_____
_____
_____
_____
_____
_____
_____
_____
_____
_____

My prayer to God:

_____
_____
_____
_____
_____
_____
_____
_____
_____
_____

Date: _____

My Bible verse of the day:

_____
_____
_____
_____
_____
_____

What this verse means in my life today:

_____
_____
_____
_____
_____
_____
_____
_____
_____
_____

My prayer to God:

_____
_____

_____
_____
_____
_____
_____
_____
_____
_____
_____

Date: _____

Deep in my heart I feel:

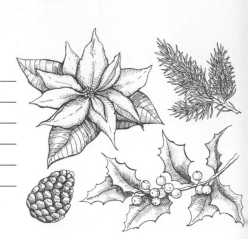

_____
_____
_____
_____
_____
_____

I thank God for:

_____
_____
_____
_____
_____
_____
_____
_____
_____
_____
_____

Today I can serve God by:

_____
_____
_____
_____
_____
_____
_____
_____
_____
_____
_____

Date: _____

My Bible verse of the day:

_____
_____
_____
_____
_____
_____

What this verse means in my life today:

_____
_____
_____
_____
_____
_____
_____
_____
_____
_____

My prayer to God:

_____
_____
_____
_____
_____
_____
_____
_____
_____
_____
_____

Date: _____

Today my heart is full of:

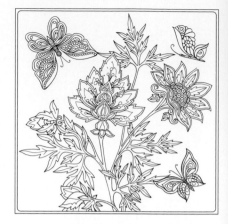

_____
_____
_____
_____
_____

I hear God reminding me:

_____
_____
_____
_____
_____
_____
_____
_____
_____
_____

I believe God is teaching me:

_____
_____
_____
_____
_____
_____
_____
_____
_____
_____
_____

Date: _____

My Bible verse of the day:

_____
_____
_____
_____
_____
_____

What this verse means in my life today:

_____
_____
_____
_____
_____
_____
_____
_____
_____
_____

My prayer to God:

_____
_____
_____
_____
_____
_____
_____
_____
_____
_____

Date: _____

Today I feel blessed because:

_____
_____
_____
_____
_____
_____

I feel God in my heart when I:

_____
_____
_____
_____
_____
_____
_____
_____
_____
_____

I have faith that God will:

_____
_____
_____
_____
_____
_____
_____
_____
_____
_____

Date: _____

My Bible verse of the day:

_____
_____
_____
_____
_____
_____

What this verse means in my life today:

_____
_____
_____
_____
_____
_____
_____
_____
_____
_____

My prayer to God:

_____
_____
_____
_____
_____
_____
_____
_____
_____
_____

Date: _____

My Bible verse of the day:

_____
_____
_____
_____
_____
_____

What this verse means in
my life today:

_____
_____
_____
_____
_____
_____
_____
_____
_____
_____
_____

My prayer to God:

_____
_____
_____
_____
_____
_____
_____
_____
_____
_____
_____

Date: _____

Deep in my heart I feel:

_____
_____
_____
_____
_____
_____

I thank God for:

_____
_____
_____
_____
_____
_____
_____
_____
_____
_____

Today I can serve God by:

_____
_____
_____
_____
_____
_____
_____
_____
_____
_____

Date: _____

My Bible verse of the day:

_____
_____
_____
_____
_____
_____

*What this verse means in
my life today:*

_____
_____
_____
_____
_____
_____
_____
_____
_____
_____

My prayer to God:

_____
_____
_____
_____
_____
_____
_____
_____
_____
_____

Date: _____

Today my heart is full of:

_____
_____
_____
_____
_____
_____

I hear God reminding me:

_____
_____
_____
_____
_____
_____
_____
_____
_____
_____

*I believe God is
teaching me:*

_____
_____
_____
_____
_____
_____
_____
_____
_____

Date: _____

My Bible verse of the day:

_____

_____

_____

_____

_____

_____

*What this verse means in
my life today:*

_____

_____

_____

_____

_____

_____

_____

_____

_____

My prayer to God:

_____

_____

_____

_____

_____

_____

_____

_____

_____

_____

Date: _____

Today I feel blessed because:

_____
_____
_____
_____
_____
_____

I feel God in my heart when I:

_____
_____
_____
_____
_____
_____
_____
_____
_____

I have faith that God will:

_____
_____
_____
_____
_____
_____
_____
_____
_____
_____
_____

Date: _____

My Bible verse of the day:

_____
_____
_____
_____
_____
_____

*What this verse means in
my life today:*

_____
_____
_____
_____
_____
_____
_____
_____
_____
_____

My prayer to God:

_____
_____
_____
_____
_____
_____
_____
_____
_____
_____

Date: _____

My Bible verse of the day:

_____
_____
_____
_____
_____
_____

What this verse means in my life today:

_____
_____
_____
_____
_____
_____
_____
_____
_____

My prayer to God:

_____
_____
_____
_____
_____
_____
_____
_____
_____
_____
_____

Date: _____

Deep in my heart I feel:
_____
_____
_____
_____
_____
_____

I thank God for:
_____
_____
_____
_____
_____
_____
_____
_____
_____
_____

Today I can serve God by:
_____
_____
_____
_____
_____
_____
_____
_____
_____
_____
_____

Date: _____

My Bible verse of the day:

_____
_____
_____
_____
_____
_____

What this verse means in my life today:

_____
_____
_____
_____
_____
_____
_____
_____
_____
_____

My prayer to God:

_____
_____
_____
_____
_____
_____
_____
_____
_____
_____
_____
_____

Date: _____

Today my heart is full of:

_____
_____
_____
_____
_____
_____

I hear God reminding me:

_____
_____
_____
_____
_____
_____
_____
_____
_____
_____

I believe God is teaching me:

_____
_____
_____
_____
_____
_____
_____
_____
_____
_____
_____
_____

Date: _____

My Bible verse of the day:

_____
_____
_____
_____
_____
_____

What this verse means in my life today:

_____
_____
_____
_____
_____
_____
_____
_____
_____

My prayer to God:

_____
_____
_____
_____
_____
_____
_____
_____
_____
_____

Date: _____

Today I feel blessed because:

_____
_____
_____
_____
_____
_____

I feel God in my heart when I:

_____
_____
_____
_____
_____
_____
_____
_____
_____
_____

I have faith that God will:

_____
_____
_____
_____
_____
_____
_____
_____
_____
_____
_____

Date: _____

My Bible verse of the day:

_____
_____
_____
_____
_____
_____
_____

What this verse means in my life today:

_____
_____
_____
_____
_____
_____
_____
_____
_____
_____

My prayer to God:

_____
_____
_____
_____
_____
_____
_____
_____
_____
_____
_____

Date: _____

My Bible verse of the day:

_____
_____
_____
_____
_____
_____

What this verse means in
my life today:

_____
_____
_____
_____
_____
_____
_____
_____
_____
_____
_____

My prayer to God:

_____
_____
_____
_____
_____
_____
_____
_____
_____
_____
_____

Date: _____

Deep in my heart I feel:

_____
_____
_____
_____
_____
_____

I thank God for:

_____
_____
_____
_____
_____
_____
_____
_____
_____

Today I can serve God by:

_____
_____
_____
_____
_____
_____
_____
_____
_____

Date: _____

My Bible verse of the day:

_____
_____
_____
_____
_____
_____

What this verse means in
my life today:

_____
_____
_____
_____
_____
_____
_____
_____
_____
_____
_____

My prayer to God:

_____
_____
_____
_____
_____
_____
_____
_____
_____
_____
_____

Date: _____

Today my heart is full of:

_____
_____
_____
_____
_____
_____

I hear God reminding me:

_____
_____
_____
_____
_____
_____
_____
_____
_____
_____
_____

I believe God is teaching me:

_____
_____
_____
_____
_____
_____
_____
_____
_____
_____
_____
_____
_____

Date: _____

My Bible verse of the day:

_____
_____
_____
_____
_____
_____

*What this verse means in
my life today:*

_____
_____
_____
_____
_____
_____
_____
_____
_____
_____

My prayer to God:

_____
_____
_____
_____
_____
_____
_____
_____
_____

Date: _____

Today I feel blessed because:

_____
_____
_____
_____
_____
_____

I feel God in my heart when I:

_____
_____
_____
_____
_____
_____
_____
_____
_____

I have faith that
God will:

_____
_____
_____
_____
_____
_____
_____
_____

Date: _____

My Bible verse of the day:

_____
_____
_____
_____
_____

*What this verse means in
my life today:*

_____
_____
_____
_____
_____
_____
_____
_____
_____
_____

My prayer to God:

_____
_____
_____
_____
_____
_____
_____
_____
_____
_____

Date: _____

My Bible verse of the day:

_____
_____
_____
_____
_____
_____

What this verse means in my life today:

_____
_____
_____
_____
_____
_____
_____
_____
_____
_____
_____

My prayer to God:

_____
_____
_____
_____
_____
_____
_____
_____
_____
_____
_____
_____

Date: _____

Deep in my heart I feel:
_____
_____
_____
_____
_____
_____

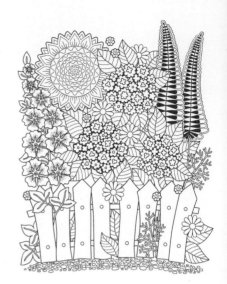

I thank God for:
_____
_____
_____
_____
_____
_____
_____
_____
_____
_____
_____

Today I can serve God by:
_____
_____
_____
_____
_____
_____
_____
_____
_____
_____
_____

Date: _____

My Bible verse of the day:

_____
_____
_____
_____
_____
_____

What this verse means in my life today:

_____
_____
_____
_____
_____
_____
_____
_____
_____

My prayer to God:

_____
_____
_____
_____
_____
_____
_____
_____
_____

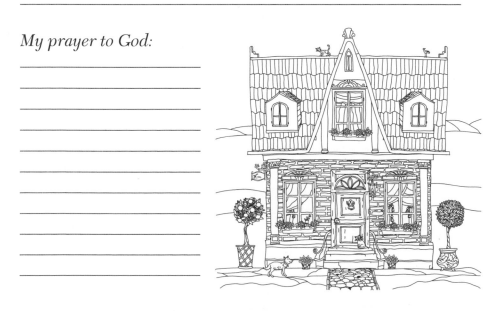

Date: _____

Today my heart is full of:

_____
_____
_____
_____
_____
_____

I hear God reminding me:

_____
_____
_____
_____
_____
_____
_____
_____
_____
_____
_____
_____

I believe God is teaching me:

_____
_____
_____
_____
_____
_____
_____
_____
_____
_____
_____
_____
_____

Date: _____

My Bible verse of the day:

_____
_____
_____
_____
_____
_____

What this verse means in my life today:

_____
_____
_____
_____
_____
_____
_____
_____
_____
_____

My prayer to God:

_____
_____
_____
_____
_____
_____
_____
_____
_____
_____
_____
_____

Date: _____

Today I feel blessed because:

_____
_____
_____
_____
_____
_____

I feel God in my heart when I:

_____
_____
_____
_____
_____
_____
_____
_____
_____

I have faith that God will:

_____
_____
_____
_____
_____
_____
_____
_____
_____
_____
_____

Date: _____

My Bible verse of the day:

_____

_____

_____

_____

_____

_____

What this verse means in my life today:

_____

_____

_____

_____

_____

_____

_____

_____

_____

_____

My prayer to God:

_____

_____

_____

_____

_____

_____

_____

_____

_____

_____

_____

Date: _____

My Bible verse of the day:

_____
_____
_____
_____
_____
_____

What this verse means in my life today:

_____
_____
_____
_____
_____
_____
_____
_____
_____
_____
_____
_____
_____

My prayer to God:

_____
_____
_____
_____
_____
_____
_____
_____
_____
_____

Date: _____

Deep in my heart I feel:

_____
_____
_____
_____
_____
_____

I thank God for:

_____
_____
_____
_____
_____
_____
_____
_____
_____
_____

Today I can serve God by:

_____
_____
_____
_____
_____
_____
_____
_____
_____
_____
_____

Date: _____

My Bible verse of the day:

_____
_____
_____
_____
_____
_____

*What this verse means in
my life today:*

_____
_____
_____
_____
_____
_____
_____
_____
_____
_____

My prayer to God:

_____
_____
_____
_____
_____
_____
_____
_____
_____
_____

Date: _____

Today my heart is full of:

_____
_____
_____
_____
_____
_____

I hear God reminding me:

_____
_____
_____
_____
_____
_____
_____
_____
_____
_____

*I believe God is
teaching me:*

_____
_____
_____
_____
_____
_____
_____
_____

Date: _____

My Bible verse of the day:

_____
_____
_____
_____
_____
_____

*What this verse means in
my life today:*

_____
_____
_____
_____
_____
_____
_____
_____
_____
_____
_____

My prayer to God:

_____
_____
_____
_____
_____
_____
_____
_____
_____
_____
_____

Date: _____

Today I feel blessed because:

_____
_____
_____
_____
_____
_____
_____

I feel God in my heart when I:

_____
_____
_____
_____
_____
_____
_____
_____
_____
_____

I have faith that God will:

_____
_____
_____
_____
_____
_____
_____
_____
_____
_____
_____
_____

Date: _____

My Bible verse of the day:

_____

_____

_____

_____

_____

_____

*What this verse means in
my life today:*

_____

_____

_____

_____

_____

_____

_____

_____

_____

_____

_____

My prayer to God:

_____

_____

_____

_____

_____

_____

_____

_____

Date: _____

My Bible verse of the day:

_____
_____
_____
_____
_____
_____

What this verse means in my life today:

_____
_____
_____
_____
_____
_____
_____
_____
_____

My prayer to God:

_____
_____
_____
_____
_____
_____
_____
_____
_____
_____
_____

Date: _____

Deep in my heart I feel:

_____
_____
_____
_____
_____
_____

I thank God for:

_____
_____
_____
_____
_____
_____
_____
_____
_____
_____

Today I can serve God by:

_____
_____
_____
_____
_____
_____
_____
_____
_____
_____

Date: _____

My Bible verse of the day:

_____
_____
_____
_____
_____
_____

What this verse means in my life today:

_____
_____
_____
_____
_____
_____
_____
_____
_____
_____

My prayer to God:

_____
_____
_____
_____
_____
_____
_____
_____
_____
_____
_____
_____
_____

Date: _____

Today my heart is full of:

_____
_____
_____
_____
_____
_____

I hear God reminding me:

_____
_____
_____
_____
_____
_____
_____
_____
_____
_____

I believe God is teaching me:

_____
_____
_____
_____
_____
_____
_____
_____
_____
_____
_____

Date: _____

My Bible verse of the day:

_____
_____
_____
_____
_____
_____

What this verse means in my life today:

_____
_____
_____
_____
_____
_____
_____
_____

My prayer to God:

Date: _____

Today I feel blessed because:

_____
_____
_____
_____
_____
_____

I feel God in my heart when I:

_____
_____
_____
_____
_____
_____
_____
_____
_____
_____
_____

I have faith that God will:

_____
_____
_____
_____
_____
_____
_____
_____
_____
_____
_____
_____
_____

Date: _____

My Bible verse of the day:

_____
_____
_____
_____
_____
_____

What this verse means in my life today:

_____
_____
_____
_____
_____
_____
_____
_____
_____

My prayer to God:

_____
_____

_____
_____
_____
_____
_____
_____
_____
_____
_____

Date: _____

My Bible verse of the day:

_____
_____
_____
_____
_____
_____

What this verse means in
my life today:

_____
_____
_____
_____
_____
_____
_____
_____
_____
_____
_____

My prayer to God:

_____
_____
_____
_____
_____
_____
_____
_____
_____
_____

Date: _____

Deep in my heart I feel:

_____
_____
_____
_____
_____
_____

I thank God for:

_____
_____
_____
_____
_____
_____
_____
_____
_____

Today I can serve God by:

_____
_____
_____
_____
_____
_____
_____
_____
_____

Date: _____

My Bible verse of the day:
_____
_____
_____
_____
_____
_____

What this verse means in
my life today:
_____
_____
_____
_____
_____
_____
_____
_____
_____
_____

My prayer to God:
_____
_____
_____
_____
_____
_____
_____
_____
_____
_____

Date: _____

Today my heart is full of:

_____
_____
_____
_____
_____
_____

I hear God reminding me:

_____
_____
_____
_____
_____
_____
_____
_____
_____

I believe God is teaching me:

_____
_____
_____
_____
_____
_____
_____
_____
_____
_____
_____
_____

Date: _____

My Bible verse of the day:

_____
_____
_____
_____
_____
_____

What this verse means in my life today:

_____
_____
_____
_____
_____
_____
_____
_____
_____
_____
_____

My prayer to God:

_____
_____
_____
_____
_____
_____
_____
_____
_____
_____
_____

Date: _____

Today I feel blessed because:

_____
_____
_____
_____
_____
_____

I feel God in my heart when I:

_____
_____
_____
_____
_____
_____
_____
_____
_____

I have faith that
God will:

_____
_____
_____
_____
_____
_____
_____
_____
_____
_____

Date: _____

My Bible verse of the day:
_____
_____
_____
_____
_____
_____

What this verse means in
my life today:
_____
_____
_____
_____
_____
_____
_____
_____
_____
_____
_____

My prayer to God:
_____
_____
_____
_____
_____
_____
_____
_____
_____
_____

Date: _____

My Bible verse of the day:

_____
_____
_____
_____
_____
_____

What this verse means in my life today:

_____
_____
_____
_____
_____
_____
_____
_____
_____

My prayer to God:

_____
_____
_____
_____
_____
_____
_____
_____
_____
_____
_____

Date: _____

Deep in my heart I feel:

_____
_____
_____
_____
_____
_____

I thank God for:

_____
_____
_____
_____
_____
_____
_____
_____
_____
_____
_____

Today I can serve God by:

_____
_____
_____
_____
_____
_____
_____
_____
_____
_____
_____

Date: _____

My Bible verse of the day:

_____
_____
_____
_____
_____
_____
_____

What this verse means in my life today:

_____
_____
_____
_____
_____
_____
_____
_____
_____
_____
_____

My prayer to God:

_____
_____
_____
_____
_____
_____
_____
_____
_____
_____
_____

Date: _____

Today my heart is full of:

_____
_____
_____
_____
_____
_____

I hear God reminding me:

_____
_____
_____
_____
_____
_____
_____
_____
_____
_____
_____

I believe God is teaching me:

_____
_____
_____
_____
_____
_____
_____
_____
_____
_____
_____
_____

Date: _____

My Bible verse of the day:

_____

_____

_____

_____

_____

_____

What this verse means in my life today:

_____

_____

_____

_____

_____

_____

_____

_____

_____

My prayer to God:

_____

_____

_____

_____

_____

_____

_____

_____

_____

_____

Date: _____

Today I feel blessed because:

_____
_____
_____
_____
_____
_____

I feel God in my heart when I:

_____
_____
_____
_____
_____
_____
_____
_____
_____
_____
_____

I have faith that God will:

_____
_____
_____
_____
_____
_____
_____
_____
_____
_____
_____
_____

Date: _____

My Bible verse of the day:

_____
_____
_____
_____
_____
_____
_____

What this verse means in my life today:

_____
_____
_____
_____
_____
_____
_____
_____
_____
_____

My prayer to God:

_____
_____
_____
_____
_____
_____
_____
_____
_____
_____
_____

Date: _____

My Bible verse of the day:

_____
_____
_____
_____
_____
_____

What this verse means in
my life today:

_____
_____
_____
_____
_____
_____
_____
_____
_____
_____

My prayer to God:

_____
_____
_____
_____
_____
_____
_____
_____
_____
_____

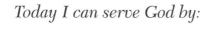

Date: _____

Deep in my heart I feel:

_____
_____
_____
_____
_____
_____

I thank God for:

_____
_____
_____
_____
_____
_____
_____
_____

Today I can serve God by:

_____
_____
_____
_____
_____
_____
_____
_____
_____
_____

Date: _____

My Bible verse of the day:

_____
_____
_____
_____
_____
_____

What this verse means in
my life today:

_____
_____
_____
_____
_____
_____
_____
_____
_____
_____

My prayer to God:

_____
_____
_____
_____
_____
_____
_____
_____
_____
_____

Date: _____

Today my heart is full of:

_____
_____
_____
_____
_____
_____

I hear God reminding me:

_____
_____
_____
_____
_____
_____
_____
_____
_____

I believe God is teaching me:

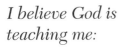

_____
_____
_____
_____
_____
_____
_____
_____

Date: _____

My Bible verse of the day:

_____
_____
_____
_____
_____
_____

What this verse means in my life today:

_____
_____
_____
_____
_____
_____
_____
_____
_____
_____
_____

My prayer to God:

_____
_____
_____
_____
_____
_____
_____
_____
_____
_____
_____
_____

Date: _____

Today I feel blessed because:

_____
_____
_____
_____
_____
_____

I feel God in my heart when I:

_____
_____
_____
_____
_____
_____
_____
_____
_____

I have faith that God will:

_____
_____
_____
_____
_____
_____
_____
_____
_____
_____
_____
_____

Date: _____

My Bible verse of the day:

_____
_____
_____
_____
_____
_____

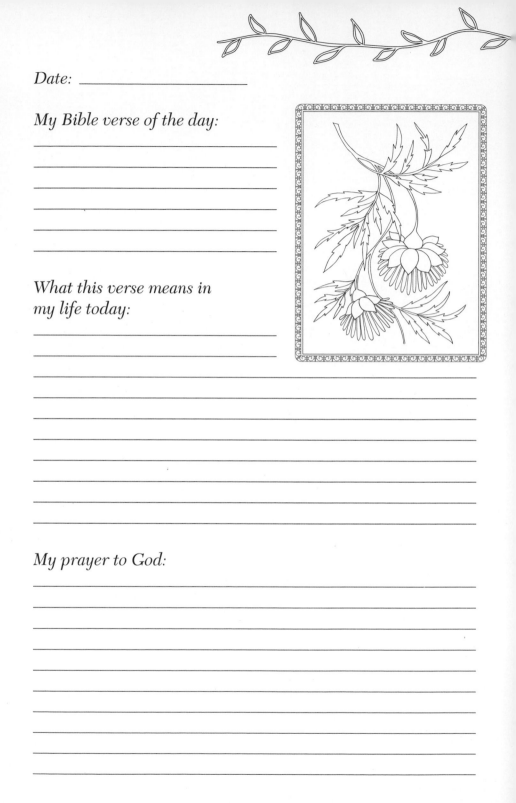

*What this verse means in
my life today:*

_____
_____
_____
_____
_____
_____
_____
_____
_____
_____

My prayer to God:

_____
_____
_____
_____
_____
_____
_____
_____
_____
_____

Date: _____

My Bible verse of the day:

_____
_____
_____
_____
_____
_____

What this verse means in my life today:

_____
_____
_____
_____
_____
_____
_____
_____
_____
_____

My prayer to God:

_____
_____
_____
_____
_____
_____
_____
_____
_____
_____

Date: _____

Deep in my heart I feel:

_____
_____
_____
_____
_____
_____

I thank God for:

_____
_____
_____

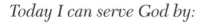

_____
_____
_____
_____
_____
_____

Today I can serve God by:

_____
_____
_____
_____
_____
_____
_____
_____
_____
_____
_____

Date: _____

My Bible verse of the day:

_____
_____
_____
_____
_____
_____

What this verse means in my life today:

_____
_____
_____
_____
_____
_____
_____
_____
_____

My prayer to God:

_____
_____
_____
_____
_____
_____
_____
_____
_____
_____
_____

Date: _____

Today my heart is full of:

_____
_____
_____
_____
_____
_____

I hear God reminding me:

_____
_____
_____
_____
_____
_____
_____
_____
_____
_____
_____

I believe God is teaching me:

_____
_____
_____
_____
_____
_____
_____
_____
_____
_____
_____
_____
_____

Date: _____

My Bible verse of the day:

_____
_____
_____
_____
_____
_____

What this verse means in my life today:

_____
_____
_____
_____
_____
_____
_____
_____
_____
_____

My prayer to God:

_____
_____
_____
_____
_____
_____
_____
_____
_____
_____
_____

Date: _____

Today I feel blessed because:

_____
_____
_____
_____
_____
_____

I feel God in my heart when I:

_____
_____
_____
_____

_____
_____
_____
_____
_____

I have faith that God will:

_____
_____
_____
_____
_____
_____
_____
_____
_____
_____
_____
_____
_____

Date: _____

My Bible verse of the day:

_____
_____
_____
_____
_____
_____

What this verse means in my life today:

_____
_____
_____
_____
_____
_____
_____
_____
_____

My prayer to God:

_____
_____
_____
_____
_____
_____
_____
_____
_____
_____
_____

Date: _____

My Bible verse of the day:

_____
_____
_____
_____
_____

What this verse means in my life today:

_____
_____
_____
_____
_____
_____
_____
_____
_____
_____

My prayer to God:

_____
_____
_____
_____
_____
_____
_____
_____
_____
_____

Date: _____

Deep in my heart I feel:

_____
_____
_____
_____
_____
_____

I thank God for:

_____
_____
_____
_____
_____
_____
_____
_____
_____
_____

Today I can serve God by:

_____
_____
_____
_____
_____
_____
_____
_____
_____

Date: _____

My Bible verse of the day:

_____
_____
_____
_____
_____
_____

What this verse means in
my life today:

_____
_____
_____
_____
_____
_____
_____
_____
_____
_____
_____

My prayer to God:

_____
_____
_____
_____
_____
_____
_____
_____
_____
_____
_____

Date: _____

Today my heart is full of:

_____
_____
_____
_____
_____
_____

I hear God reminding me:

_____
_____
_____
_____
_____
_____
_____
_____
_____
_____

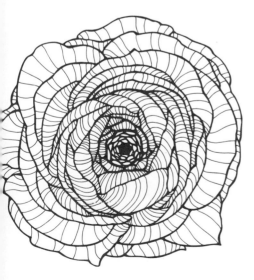

I believe God is teaching me:

_____
_____
_____
_____
_____
_____
_____
_____
_____
_____

Date: _____

My Bible verse of the day:

_____
_____
_____
_____
_____
_____

*What this verse means in
my life today:*

_____
_____
_____
_____
_____
_____
_____
_____
_____
_____
_____

My prayer to God:

_____
_____
_____
_____
_____
_____
_____
_____
_____
_____

Date: _____

Today I feel blessed because:

_____
_____
_____
_____
_____
_____

I feel God in my heart when I:

_____
_____
_____
_____
_____
_____
_____
_____
_____
_____

I have faith that
God will:

_____
_____
_____
_____
_____
_____
_____
_____
_____
_____

Date: _____

My Bible verse of the day:

_____
_____
_____
_____
_____
_____

*What this verse means in
my life today:*

_____
_____
_____
_____
_____
_____
_____
_____
_____
_____
_____

My prayer to God:

_____
_____
_____
_____
_____
_____
_____
_____
_____
_____
_____

Date: _____

My Bible verse of the day:

_____
_____
_____
_____
_____
_____

What this verse means in my life today:

_____
_____
_____
_____
_____
_____
_____
_____
_____
_____

My prayer to God:

_____
_____
_____
_____
_____
_____
_____
_____
_____
_____
_____
_____

Date: _____

Deep in my heart I feel:

_____
_____
_____
_____
_____
_____

I thank God for:

_____
_____
_____
_____
_____
_____
_____
_____
_____
_____
_____
_____

Today I can serve God by:

_____
_____
_____
_____
_____
_____
_____
_____
_____
_____
_____
_____
_____

Date: _____

My Bible verse of the day:

_____
_____
_____
_____
_____
_____

What this verse means in my life today:

_____
_____
_____
_____
_____
_____
_____
_____
_____
_____
_____

My prayer to God:

_____
_____
_____
_____
_____
_____
_____
_____
_____
_____
_____
_____

Date: _____

Today my heart is full of:

_____
_____
_____
_____
_____

I hear God reminding me:

_____
_____
_____
_____
_____
_____
_____
_____
_____
_____

I believe God is teaching me:

_____
_____
_____
_____
_____
_____
_____
_____
_____
_____
_____

Date: _____

My Bible verse of the day:

_____
_____
_____
_____
_____
_____

What this verse means in my life today:

_____
_____
_____
_____
_____
_____
_____
_____
_____
_____

My prayer to God:

_____
_____
_____
_____
_____
_____
_____
_____
_____
_____
_____
_____

Date: _____

Today I feel blessed because:

_____
_____
_____
_____
_____
_____

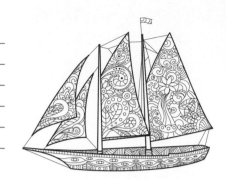

I feel God in my heart when I:

_____
_____
_____
_____
_____
_____
_____
_____
_____
_____

I have faith that God will:

_____
_____
_____
_____
_____
_____
_____
_____
_____
_____
_____
_____

Date: _____

My Bible verse of the day:

_____
_____
_____
_____
_____
_____

What this verse means in my life today:

_____
_____
_____
_____
_____
_____
_____
_____
_____

My prayer to God:

_____
_____
_____
_____
_____
_____
_____
_____
_____

Date: _____

My Bible verse of the day:

_____
_____
_____
_____
_____
_____

*What this verse means in
my life today:*

_____
_____
_____
_____
_____
_____
_____
_____
_____

My prayer to God:

_____
_____
_____
_____
_____
_____
_____
_____
_____

Date: _____

Deep in my heart I feel:

_____
_____
_____
_____
_____
_____

I thank God for:

_____
_____
_____
_____
_____
_____
_____
_____

Today I can serve God by:

_____
_____
_____
_____
_____
_____
_____
_____
_____
_____
_____

Date: _____

My Bible verse of the day:

_____
_____
_____
_____
_____
_____

What this verse means in my life today:

_____
_____
_____
_____
_____
_____
_____
_____
_____
_____

My prayer to God:

_____
_____
_____
_____
_____
_____
_____
_____
_____

Date: _____

Today my heart is full of:

_____
_____
_____
_____
_____
_____

I hear God reminding me:

_____
_____
_____
_____
_____
_____
_____
_____
_____

I believe God is teaching me:

_____
_____
_____
_____
_____
_____
_____
_____
_____
_____
_____
_____

Date: _____

My Bible verse of the day:

_____
_____
_____
_____
_____

What this verse means in
my life today:

_____
_____
_____
_____
_____
_____
_____
_____
_____
_____
_____

My prayer to God:

_____
_____
_____
_____
_____
_____
_____
_____
_____
_____

Date: _____

Today I feel blessed because:

_____
_____
_____
_____
_____
_____

I feel God in my heart when I:

_____
_____
_____
_____
_____
_____
_____
_____
_____

I have faith that God will:

_____
_____
_____
_____
_____
_____
_____
_____
_____
_____
_____
_____

Date: _____

My Bible verse of the day:

_____
_____
_____
_____
_____
_____

What this verse means in my life today:

_____
_____
_____

_____
_____
_____
_____
_____
_____
_____
_____

My prayer to God:

_____
_____
_____
_____
_____
_____
_____
_____
_____
_____
_____

Date: _____

My Bible verse of the day:

_____
_____
_____
_____
_____
_____

What this verse means in my life today:

_____
_____
_____
_____
_____
_____
_____
_____
_____
_____
_____

My prayer to God:

_____
_____
_____
_____
_____
_____
_____
_____
_____
_____

Date: _____

Deep in my heart I feel:

_____
_____
_____
_____
_____
_____

I thank God for:

_____
_____
_____
_____
_____
_____
_____
_____
_____
_____

Today I can serve God by:

_____
_____
_____
_____
_____
_____
_____
_____
_____
_____
_____
_____

Date: _____

My Bible verse of the day:

_____
_____
_____
_____
_____
_____

What this verse means in my life today:

_____
_____
_____
_____
_____
_____
_____
_____
_____
_____

My prayer to God:

_____
_____
_____
_____
_____
_____
_____
_____
_____
_____
_____

Date: _____

Today my heart is full of:

_____
_____
_____
_____
_____
_____

I hear God reminding me:

_____
_____
_____
_____
_____
_____
_____
_____
_____
_____

I believe God is teaching me:

_____
_____
_____
_____
_____
_____
_____
_____
_____
_____
_____
_____

Date: _____

My Bible verse of the day:

_____
_____
_____
_____
_____
_____

What this verse means in my life today:

_____
_____
_____
_____
_____
_____
_____
_____
_____
_____

My prayer to God:

_____
_____
_____
_____
_____
_____
_____
_____
_____
_____
_____

Date: _____

Today I feel blessed because:

_____
_____
_____
_____
_____

I feel God in my heart when I:

_____
_____
_____
_____
_____
_____
_____
_____
_____
_____

I have faith that God will:

_____
_____
_____
_____
_____
_____
_____
_____
_____
_____
_____
_____

Date: _____

My Bible verse of the day:

_____
_____
_____
_____
_____
_____

What this verse means in my life today:

_____
_____
_____
_____
_____
_____
_____
_____
_____

My prayer to God:

_____
_____
_____
_____
_____
_____
_____
_____
_____
_____
_____
_____
_____

Date: _____

My Bible verse of the day:

_____
_____
_____
_____
_____
_____

What this verse means in
my life today:

_____
_____
_____
_____
_____
_____
_____
_____
_____
_____
_____

My prayer to God:

_____
_____
_____
_____
_____
_____
_____
_____
_____
_____
_____

Date: _____

Deep in my heart I feel:

_____
_____
_____
_____
_____
_____

I thank God for:

_____
_____
_____
_____
_____
_____
_____
_____
_____

Today I can serve God by:

_____
_____
_____
_____
_____
_____
_____
_____
_____

Date: _____

My Bible verse of the day:

_____
_____
_____
_____
_____
_____

What this verse means in my life today:

_____
_____
_____
_____
_____
_____
_____
_____
_____
_____
_____

My prayer to God:

_____
_____
_____
_____
_____
_____
_____
_____
_____
_____
_____

Date: _____

Today my heart is full of:

_____
_____
_____
_____
_____
_____

I hear God reminding me:

_____
_____
_____
_____
_____
_____
_____
_____
_____

I believe God is teaching me:

_____
_____
_____
_____
_____
_____
_____
_____
_____
_____
_____
_____

Date: _____

My Bible verse of the day:
_____
_____
_____
_____
_____
_____

What this verse means in
my life today:
_____
_____
_____
_____
_____
_____
_____
_____
_____
_____
_____

My prayer to God:
_____
_____
_____
_____
_____
_____
_____
_____
_____
_____
_____

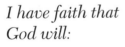

Date: _____

Today I feel blessed because:

_____
_____
_____
_____
_____
_____

I feel God in my heart when I:

_____
_____
_____
_____
_____
_____
_____
_____
_____

I have faith that
God will:

_____
_____
_____
_____
_____
_____
_____
_____
_____
_____

Date: _____

My Bible verse of the day:

_____
_____
_____
_____
_____
_____

What this verse means in
my life today:

_____
_____
_____
_____
_____
_____
_____
_____
_____
_____

My prayer to God:

_____
_____
_____
_____
_____
_____
_____
_____
_____
_____

Date: _____

My Bible verse of the day:

_____
_____
_____
_____
_____
_____

What this verse means in my life today:

_____
_____
_____
_____
_____
_____
_____
_____
_____
_____

My prayer to God:

_____
_____
_____
_____
_____
_____
_____
_____
_____
_____
_____
_____

Date: _____

Deep in my heart I feel:

_____
_____
_____
_____
_____
_____

I thank God for:

_____
_____
_____
_____
_____
_____
_____
_____
_____
_____
_____

Today I can serve God by:

_____
_____
_____
_____
_____
_____
_____
_____
_____
_____
_____
_____

Date: _____

My Bible verse of the day:

_____
_____
_____
_____
_____
_____

What this verse means in my life today:

_____
_____
_____
_____
_____
_____
_____
_____
_____

My prayer to God:

_____
_____
_____
_____
_____
_____
_____
_____
_____

Date: _____

Today my heart is full of:

_____
_____
_____
_____
_____
_____

I hear God reminding me:

_____
_____
_____
_____
_____
_____
_____
_____
_____
_____
_____

I believe God is teaching me:

_____
_____
_____
_____
_____
_____
_____
_____
_____
_____
_____
_____

Date: _____

My Bible verse of the day:

_____
_____
_____
_____
_____
_____
_____

What this verse means in my life today:

_____
_____
_____
_____
_____
_____
_____
_____
_____
_____

My prayer to God:

_____
_____
_____
_____
_____
_____
_____
_____
_____
_____
_____
_____

Date: _____

Today I feel blessed because:

_____
_____
_____
_____
_____
_____

I feel God in my heart when I:

_____
_____
_____
_____
_____
_____
_____
_____
_____
_____
_____

I have faith that God will:

_____
_____
_____
_____
_____
_____
_____
_____
_____
_____
_____
_____
_____

Date: _____

My Bible verse of the day:

_____
_____
_____
_____
_____
_____

What this verse means in my life today:

_____
_____
_____
_____
_____
_____
_____
_____
_____
_____

My prayer to God:

_____
_____
_____
_____
_____
_____
_____
_____
_____

Date: _____

My Bible verse of the day:

_____
_____
_____
_____
_____

What this verse means in my life today:

_____
_____
_____
_____
_____
_____
_____
_____
_____
_____
_____

My prayer to God:

_____
_____
_____
_____
_____
_____
_____
_____
_____

Date: _____

Deep in my heart I feel:

_____
_____
_____
_____
_____
_____

I thank God for:

_____
_____
_____
_____
_____
_____
_____
_____
_____

Today I can serve God by:

_____
_____
_____
_____
_____
_____
_____
_____
_____
_____
_____

Date: _____

My Bible verse of the day:

_____
_____
_____
_____
_____
_____

What this verse means in my life today:

_____
_____
_____
_____
_____
_____
_____
_____
_____
_____
_____

My prayer to God:

_____
_____
_____
_____
_____
_____
_____
_____
_____
_____
_____

Date: _____

Today my heart is full of:

_____
_____
_____
_____
_____
_____

I hear God reminding me:

_____
_____
_____
_____
_____
_____
_____
_____
_____

*I believe God is
teaching me:*

_____
_____
_____
_____
_____
_____
_____
_____

Date: _____

My Bible verse of the day:

_____
_____
_____
_____
_____
_____

What this verse means in my life today:

_____
_____
_____
_____
_____
_____
_____
_____
_____
_____
_____

My prayer to God:

_____
_____
_____
_____
_____
_____
_____
_____
_____
_____
_____

Date: _____

Today I feel blessed because:

_____
_____
_____
_____
_____
_____

I feel God in my heart when I:

_____
_____
_____
_____
_____
_____
_____
_____
_____
_____

I have faith that God will:

_____
_____
_____
_____
_____
_____
_____
_____
_____
_____

Date: _____

My Bible verse of the day:
_____
_____
_____
_____
_____

What this verse means in my life today:
_____
_____
_____
_____
_____
_____
_____
_____
_____
_____
_____

My prayer to God:
_____
_____
_____
_____
_____
_____
_____
_____
_____
_____
_____

Date: _____

My Bible verse of the day:

_____
_____
_____
_____
_____
_____

What this verse means in my life today:

_____
_____
_____
_____
_____
_____
_____
_____
_____

My prayer to God:

_____
_____
_____
_____
_____
_____
_____
_____
_____

Date: _____

Deep in my heart I feel:

_____
_____
_____
_____
_____
_____

I thank God for:

_____
_____
_____
_____
_____
_____
_____
_____
_____
_____

Today I can serve God by:

_____
_____
_____
_____
_____
_____
_____
_____
_____
_____
_____

Date: _____

My Bible verse of the day:

_____
_____
_____
_____
_____
_____

What this verse means in my life today:

_____
_____
_____
_____
_____
_____
_____
_____
_____
_____

My prayer to God:

_____
_____
_____
_____
_____
_____
_____
_____
_____
_____
_____
_____

Date: _____

Today my heart is full of:

_____
_____
_____
_____
_____

I hear God reminding me:

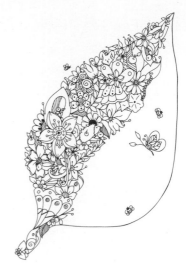

_____
_____
_____
_____

_____
_____
_____
_____
_____
_____

I believe God is teaching me:

_____
_____
_____
_____
_____
_____
_____
_____
_____
_____
_____

Date: _____

My Bible verse of the day:

_____
_____
_____
_____
_____
_____
_____

What this verse means in my life today:

_____
_____
_____
_____
_____
_____
_____
_____
_____
_____
_____

My prayer to God:

_____
_____
_____
_____
_____
_____
_____
_____
_____
_____
_____

Date: _____

Today I feel blessed because:

_____

_____

_____

_____

_____

_____

I feel God in my heart when I:

_____

_____

_____

_____

_____

_____

_____

_____

_____

_____

I have faith that God will:

_____

_____

_____

_____

_____

_____

_____

_____

_____

_____

_____

_____

Date: _____

My Bible verse of the day:

_____
_____
_____
_____
_____
_____

What this verse means in my life today:

_____
_____
_____
_____
_____
_____
_____
_____
_____
_____

My prayer to God:

_____
_____
_____
_____
_____
_____
_____
_____
_____
_____
_____

Date: _____

My Bible verse of the day:

_____
_____
_____
_____
_____
_____

What this verse means in my life today:

_____
_____
_____
_____
_____
_____
_____
_____
_____
_____
_____
_____

My prayer to God:

_____
_____
_____
_____
_____
_____
_____
_____
_____
_____
_____
_____
_____

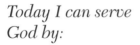

Date: _____

Deep in my heart I feel:

_____
_____
_____
_____
_____
_____
_____

I thank God for:

_____
_____
_____
_____
_____
_____
_____
_____
_____
_____

*Today I can serve
God by:*

_____
_____
_____
_____
_____
_____
_____
_____
_____
_____

Date: _____

My Bible verse of the day:

_____
_____
_____
_____
_____
_____

What this verse means in my life today:

_____
_____
_____
_____
_____
_____
_____
_____
_____
_____
_____

My prayer to God:

_____
_____
_____
_____
_____
_____
_____
_____
_____
_____

Date: _____

Today my heart is full of:

_____
_____
_____
_____
_____
_____

I hear God reminding me:

_____
_____
_____
_____
_____
_____
_____
_____
_____

I believe God is teaching me:

_____
_____
_____
_____
_____
_____
_____
_____
_____
_____
_____
_____
_____

Date: _____

My Bible verse of the day:

_____
_____
_____
_____
_____
_____

What this verse means in my life today:

_____
_____
_____
_____
_____
_____
_____
_____
_____
_____

My prayer to God:

_____
_____
_____
_____
_____
_____
_____
_____
_____
_____
_____

Date: _____

Today I feel blessed because:

_____

_____

_____

_____

_____

_____

I feel God in my heart when I:

_____

_____

_____

_____

_____

_____

_____

_____

_____

_____

I have faith that God will:

_____

_____

_____

_____

_____

_____

_____

_____

_____

_____

_____

_____

Date: _____

My Bible verse of the day:

_____
_____
_____
_____
_____
_____

What this verse means in
my life today:

_____
_____
_____
_____
_____
_____
_____
_____
_____
_____
_____

My prayer to God:

_____
_____
_____
_____
_____
_____
_____
_____
_____
_____
_____

Date: _____

My Bible verse of the day:

_____
_____
_____
_____
_____
_____

What this verse means in my life today:

_____
_____
_____
_____
_____
_____
_____
_____

My prayer to God:

_____
_____
_____
_____
_____
_____
_____
_____
_____
_____
_____
_____

Date: _____

Deep in my heart I feel:

_____
_____
_____
_____
_____
_____

I thank God for:

_____
_____
_____
_____
_____
_____
_____
_____
_____
_____

Today I can serve God by:

_____
_____
_____
_____
_____
_____
_____
_____
_____
_____
_____
_____

Date: _____

My Bible verse of the day:

_____
_____
_____
_____
_____
_____

What this verse means in my life today:

_____
_____
_____
_____
_____
_____
_____
_____
_____

My prayer to God:

_____
_____
_____
_____
_____
_____
_____
_____
_____
_____

Date: _____

Today my heart is full of:

_____
_____
_____
_____
_____
_____

I hear God reminding me:

_____
_____
_____
_____
_____
_____
_____
_____
_____
_____

I believe God is teaching me:

_____
_____
_____
_____
_____
_____
_____
_____
_____
_____
_____
_____

Date: _____

My Bible verse of the day:

_____
_____
_____
_____
_____
_____

What this verse means in my life today:

_____
_____
_____
_____
_____
_____
_____
_____
_____

My prayer to God:

_____
_____
_____
_____
_____
_____
_____
_____
_____
_____
_____

Date: _____

Today I feel blessed because:

_____
_____
_____
_____
_____
_____

I feel God in my heart when I:

_____
_____
_____
_____

_____
_____
_____
_____
_____
_____

I have faith that God will:

_____
_____
_____
_____
_____
_____
_____
_____
_____
_____
_____

Date: _____

My Bible verse of the day:

_____
_____
_____
_____
_____
_____
_____

What this verse means in my life today:

_____
_____
_____
_____
_____
_____
_____
_____
_____
_____

My prayer to God:

_____
_____
_____
_____
_____
_____
_____
_____
_____
_____
_____

Date: _____

My Bible verse of the day:

_____
_____
_____
_____
_____
_____

What this verse means in
my life today:

_____
_____
_____
_____
_____
_____
_____
_____
_____
_____

My prayer to God:

_____
_____
_____
_____
_____
_____
_____
_____
_____
_____

Date: _____

Deep in my heart I feel:

_____
_____
_____
_____
_____
_____

I thank God for:

_____
_____
_____
_____
_____
_____
_____
_____
_____

Today I can serve God by:

_____
_____
_____
_____
_____
_____
_____
_____
_____
_____

Date:

My Bible verse of the day:

_____
_____
_____
_____
_____
_____

*What this verse means in
my life today:*

_____
_____
_____
_____
_____
_____
_____
_____
_____
_____
_____

My prayer to God:

_____
_____
_____
_____
_____
_____
_____
_____
_____
_____

Date: _____

Today my heart is full of:

_____
_____
_____
_____
_____
_____
_____

I hear God reminding me:

_____
_____
_____
_____
_____
_____
_____
_____
_____
_____

*I believe God is
teaching me:*

_____
_____
_____
_____
_____
_____
_____
_____
_____
_____

Date: _____

My Bible verse of the day:
_____
_____
_____
_____
_____
_____

What this verse means in my life today:
_____
_____
_____
_____
_____
_____
_____
_____
_____
_____
_____

My prayer to God:
_____
_____
_____
_____
_____
_____
_____
_____
_____
_____

Date: _____

Today I feel blessed because:

_____
_____
_____
_____
_____
_____

I feel God in my heart when I:

_____
_____
_____
_____
_____
_____
_____
_____
_____

I have faith that God will:

_____
_____
_____
_____
_____
_____
_____
_____
_____
_____
_____

Date: _____

My Bible verse of the day:

_____
_____
_____
_____
_____
_____

What this verse means in my life today:

_____
_____
_____
_____
_____
_____
_____
_____
_____
_____
_____

My prayer to God:

_____
_____
_____
_____
_____
_____
_____
_____
_____
_____
_____
_____

Date: _____

My Bible verse of the day:

_____
_____
_____
_____
_____
_____
_____

What this verse means in my life today:

_____
_____
_____
_____
_____
_____
_____
_____
_____
_____
_____

My prayer to God:

_____
_____
_____
_____
_____
_____
_____
_____
_____
_____
_____

Date: _____

Deep in my heart I feel:

_____
_____
_____
_____
_____
_____

I thank God for:

_____
_____
_____
_____
_____
_____
_____
_____
_____
_____

Today I can serve God by:

_____
_____
_____
_____
_____
_____
_____
_____
_____
_____
_____

Date: _____

My Bible verse of the day:

_____
_____
_____
_____
_____
_____

What this verse means in my life today:

_____
_____
_____
_____
_____
_____
_____
_____
_____
_____

My prayer to God:

_____
_____
_____
_____
_____
_____
_____
_____
_____
_____
_____

Date: _____

Today my heart is full of:

_____
_____
_____
_____
_____
_____

I hear God reminding me:

_____
_____
_____
_____
_____
_____
_____
_____
_____
_____

I believe God is teaching me:

_____
_____
_____
_____
_____
_____
_____
_____
_____
_____
_____

Date: _____

My Bible verse of the day:

_____
_____
_____
_____
_____
_____

What this verse means in my life today:

_____
_____
_____
_____
_____
_____
_____
_____
_____

My prayer to God:

_____
_____
_____
_____
_____
_____
_____
_____
_____
_____
_____

Date: _____

Today I feel blessed because:

_____
_____
_____
_____
_____
_____

I feel God in my heart when I:

_____
_____
_____

_____
_____
_____
_____
_____
_____
_____
_____

I have faith that God will:

_____
_____
_____
_____
_____
_____
_____
_____
_____
_____
_____
_____

Date: _____

My Bible verse of the day:

_____
_____
_____
_____
_____
_____

What this verse means in my life today:

_____
_____
_____
_____
_____
_____
_____
_____
_____

My prayer to God:

_____
_____
_____
_____
_____
_____
_____
_____
_____
_____
_____

Date: _____

My Bible verse of the day:

_____
_____
_____
_____
_____
_____

What this verse means in my life today:

_____
_____
_____
_____
_____
_____
_____
_____
_____
_____
_____

My prayer to God:

_____
_____
_____
_____
_____
_____
_____
_____
_____
_____
_____

Date: _____

Deep in my heart I feel:

_____
_____
_____
_____
_____
_____

I thank God for:

_____
_____
_____
_____
_____
_____
_____
_____
_____

Today I can serve God by:

_____
_____
_____
_____
_____
_____
_____
_____
_____

Date: _____

My Bible verse of the day:

_____
_____
_____
_____
_____
_____

What this verse means in
my life today:

_____
_____
_____
_____
_____
_____
_____
_____
_____
_____

My prayer to God:

_____
_____
_____
_____
_____
_____
_____
_____
_____

Date: _____

Today my heart is full of:

_____
_____
_____
_____
_____
_____

I hear God reminding me:

_____
_____
_____
_____
_____
_____
_____
_____
_____
_____

I believe God is teaching me:

_____
_____
_____
_____
_____
_____
_____
_____
_____
_____
_____
_____

Date: _____

My Bible verse of the day:

_____
_____
_____
_____
_____
_____

What this verse means in my life today:

_____
_____
_____
_____
_____
_____
_____
_____
_____
_____
_____

My prayer to God:

_____
_____
_____
_____
_____
_____
_____
_____
_____
_____
_____

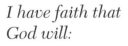

Date: _____

Today I feel blessed because:

_____
_____
_____
_____
_____
_____

I feel God in my heart when I:

_____
_____
_____
_____
_____
_____
_____
_____
_____

*I have faith that
God will:*

_____
_____
_____
_____
_____
_____
_____
_____

Date: _____

My Bible verse of the day:

_____
_____
_____
_____
_____
_____

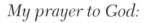

What this verse means in
my life today:

_____
_____
_____
_____
_____
_____
_____
_____
_____
_____

My prayer to God:

_____
_____
_____
_____
_____
_____
_____
_____
_____
_____

Date: _____

My Bible verse of the day:

_____
_____
_____
_____
_____
_____

What this verse means in my life today:

_____
_____
_____
_____
_____
_____
_____
_____
_____
_____
_____

My prayer to God:

_____
_____
_____
_____
_____
_____
_____
_____
_____
_____
_____
_____
_____

Date: _____

Deep in my heart I feel:

_____
_____
_____
_____
_____
_____

I thank God for:

_____
_____
_____
_____
_____
_____
_____
_____
_____
_____
_____

Today I can serve God by:

_____
_____
_____
_____
_____
_____
_____
_____
_____
_____
_____
_____

Date: _____

My Bible verse of the day:

_____
_____
_____
_____
_____
_____

What this verse means in my life today:

_____
_____
_____
_____
_____
_____
_____
_____
_____
_____

My prayer to God:

_____
_____
_____
_____
_____
_____
_____
_____
_____
_____

Date: _____

Today my heart is full of:

_____
_____
_____
_____
_____
_____

I hear God reminding me:

_____
_____
_____
_____

_____
_____
_____
_____
_____
_____

I believe God is teaching me:

_____
_____
_____
_____
_____
_____
_____
_____
_____
_____
_____

Date: _____

My Bible verse of the day:

_____
_____
_____
_____
_____
_____

What this verse means in my life today:

_____
_____
_____
_____
_____
_____
_____
_____
_____

My prayer to God:

_____
_____
_____
_____
_____
_____
_____
_____
_____
_____
_____

Date: _____

Today I feel blessed because:

_____
_____
_____
_____
_____
_____

I feel God in my heart when I:

_____
_____
_____
_____
_____
_____
_____
_____
_____
_____
_____

I have faith that God will:

_____
_____
_____
_____
_____
_____
_____
_____
_____
_____
_____
_____

Date: _____

My Bible verse of the day:

_____
_____
_____
_____
_____
_____

What this verse means in my life today:

_____
_____
_____
_____
_____
_____
_____
_____
_____

My prayer to God:

_____
_____
_____
_____
_____
_____
_____
_____
_____

Date: _____

My Bible verse of the day:

_____
_____
_____
_____
_____
_____

What this verse means in
my life today:

_____
_____
_____
_____
_____
_____
_____
_____
_____
_____
_____

My prayer to God:

_____
_____
_____
_____
_____
_____
_____
_____
_____
_____
_____

Date: _____

Deep in my heart I feel:

_____
_____
_____
_____
_____
_____

I thank God for:

_____
_____
_____
_____
_____
_____
_____
_____
_____
_____

Today I can serve God by:

_____
_____

_____
_____
_____
_____
_____
_____
_____
_____
_____

Date: _____

My Bible verse of the day:

_____
_____
_____
_____
_____
_____

What this verse means in
my life today:

_____
_____
_____
_____
_____
_____
_____
_____
_____
_____

My prayer to God:

_____
_____
_____
_____
_____
_____
_____
_____
_____
_____

Date: _____

Today my heart is full of:

_____
_____
_____
_____
_____
_____

I hear God reminding me:

_____
_____
_____
_____
_____
_____
_____
_____
_____

I believe God is teaching me:

_____
_____
_____
_____
_____
_____
_____
_____
_____

Date: _____

My Bible verse of the day:

_____
_____
_____
_____
_____

What this verse means in
my life today:

_____
_____
_____
_____
_____
_____
_____
_____
_____
_____
_____

My prayer to God:

_____
_____
_____
_____
_____
_____
_____
_____
_____
_____
_____

Date: _____

Today I feel blessed because:

_____
_____
_____
_____
_____
_____

I feel God in my heart when I:

_____
_____
_____
_____
_____
_____
_____
_____
_____

I have faith that God will:

_____
_____

_____
_____
_____
_____
_____
_____
_____
_____

Date: _____

My Bible verse of the day:

_____
_____
_____
_____
_____
_____

*What this verse means in
my life today:*

_____
_____
_____
_____
_____
_____
_____
_____
_____
_____

My prayer to God:

_____
_____
_____
_____
_____
_____
_____
_____
_____
_____
_____

Date: _____

My Bible verse of the day:

_____
_____
_____
_____
_____
_____

What this verse means in my life today:

_____
_____
_____
_____
_____
_____
_____
_____
_____

My prayer to God:

Date: _____

Deep in my heart I feel:

_____
_____
_____
_____
_____
_____

I thank God for:

_____
_____
_____
_____
_____
_____
_____
_____
_____
_____

Today I can serve God by:

_____
_____
_____
_____
_____
_____
_____
_____
_____
_____
_____

Date: _____

My Bible verse of the day:

_____
_____
_____
_____
_____
_____

What this verse means in my life today:

_____
_____
_____
_____
_____
_____
_____
_____
_____
_____

My prayer to God:

_____
_____
_____
_____
_____
_____
_____
_____
_____
_____
_____
_____
_____

Date: _____

Today my heart is full of:

_____
_____
_____
_____
_____
_____

I hear God reminding me:

_____
_____
_____
_____
_____
_____
_____
_____
_____
_____
_____

I believe God is teaching me:

_____
_____
_____
_____
_____
_____
_____
_____
_____
_____
_____
_____
_____

Date: _____

My Bible verse of the day:

_____
_____
_____
_____
_____
_____

What this verse means in my life today:

_____
_____
_____
_____
_____
_____
_____
_____
_____
_____

My prayer to God:

_____
_____
_____
_____
_____
_____
_____
_____
_____
_____

Date: _____

Today I feel blessed because:

_____
_____
_____
_____
_____
_____

I feel God in my heart when I:

_____
_____
_____
_____
_____
_____
_____
_____
_____
_____
_____

I have faith that God will:

_____
_____
_____
_____
_____
_____
_____
_____
_____
_____
_____

Date: _____

My Bible verse of the day:

_____

_____

_____

_____

_____

_____

What this verse means in my life today:

_____

_____

_____

_____

_____

_____

_____

_____

_____

My prayer to God:

_____

_____

_____

_____

_____

_____

_____

_____

_____

_____

_____

Date: _____

My Bible verse of the day:

_____
_____
_____
_____
_____
_____

What this verse means in my life today:

_____
_____
_____
_____
_____
_____
_____
_____
_____
_____
_____

My prayer to God:

_____
_____
_____
_____
_____
_____
_____
_____
_____
_____
_____

Date: _____

Deep in my heart I feel:

_____
_____
_____
_____
_____
_____

I thank God for:

_____
_____
_____
_____
_____
_____
_____
_____
_____
_____

Today I can serve God by:

_____
_____
_____
_____
_____
_____
_____
_____
_____
_____

Date: _____

My Bible verse of the day:

_____
_____
_____
_____
_____
_____

What this verse means in
my life today:

_____
_____
_____
_____
_____
_____
_____
_____
_____
_____

My prayer to God:

_____
_____
_____
_____
_____
_____
_____
_____
_____
_____

Date: _____

Today my heart is full of:

_____
_____
_____
_____
_____
_____

I hear God reminding me:

_____
_____
_____
_____
_____
_____
_____
_____
_____

I believe God is teaching me:

_____
_____
_____
_____
_____
_____
_____
_____
_____
_____
_____
_____

Date: _____

My Bible verse of the day:

_____
_____
_____
_____
_____
_____

What this verse means in
my life today:

_____
_____
_____
_____
_____
_____
_____
_____
_____
_____

My prayer to God:

_____
_____
_____
_____
_____
_____
_____
_____
_____
_____

Date: _____

Today I feel blessed because:

_____
_____
_____
_____
_____
_____

I feel God in my heart when I:

_____
_____
_____
_____
_____
_____
_____
_____
_____

I have faith that God will:

_____
_____
_____
_____
_____
_____
_____
_____
_____
_____
_____

Date: _____

My Bible verse of the day:

_____
_____
_____
_____
_____
_____

What this verse means in
my life today:

_____
_____
_____
_____
_____
_____
_____
_____
_____
_____

My prayer to God:

_____
_____
_____
_____
_____
_____
_____
_____
_____
_____

Date: _____

My Bible verse of the day:

_____
_____
_____
_____
_____
_____

What this verse means in my life today:

_____
_____
_____
_____
_____
_____
_____
_____
_____
_____

My prayer to God:

_____
_____
_____
_____
_____
_____
_____
_____
_____
_____

Date: _____

Deep in my heart I feel:

_____
_____
_____
_____
_____
_____

I thank God for:

_____
_____
_____
_____
_____
_____
_____
_____
_____
_____
_____

Today I can serve God by:

_____
_____
_____
_____
_____
_____
_____
_____
_____
_____
_____
_____

Date: _____

My Bible verse of the day:

_____
_____
_____
_____
_____
_____

What this verse means in my life today:

_____
_____
_____
_____
_____
_____
_____
_____
_____
_____
_____

My prayer to God:

_____
_____
_____
_____
_____
_____
_____
_____
_____
_____

Date: _____

Today my heart is full of:

_____
_____
_____
_____
_____

I hear God reminding me:

_____
_____
_____
_____
_____
_____
_____
_____
_____

I believe God is teaching me:

_____
_____
_____
_____
_____
_____
_____
_____
_____
_____
_____

Date: _____

My Bible verse of the day:

_____
_____
_____
_____
_____
_____

What this verse means in my life today:

_____
_____
_____
_____
_____
_____
_____
_____
_____
_____

My prayer to God:

_____
_____
_____
_____
_____
_____
_____
_____
_____
_____
_____

Date: _____

Today I feel blessed because:

_____
_____
_____
_____
_____
_____

I feel God in my heart when I:

_____
_____
_____
_____

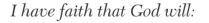

_____
_____
_____
_____
_____
_____

I have faith that God will:

_____
_____
_____
_____
_____
_____
_____
_____
_____
_____
_____

Date: _____

My Bible verse of the day:

_____
_____
_____
_____
_____
_____

What this verse means in my life today:

_____
_____
_____
_____
_____
_____
_____
_____
_____
_____

My prayer to God:

_____
_____
_____
_____
_____
_____
_____
_____
_____
_____

Date: _____

My Bible verse of the day:

_____
_____
_____
_____
_____
_____

*What this verse means in
my life today:*

_____
_____
_____
_____
_____
_____
_____
_____
_____
_____

My prayer to God:

_____
_____
_____
_____
_____
_____
_____
_____
_____
_____

Date: _____

Deep in my heart I feel:

_____
_____
_____
_____
_____
_____

I thank God for:

_____
_____
_____
_____
_____
_____
_____
_____

Today I can serve God by:

_____
_____
_____
_____
_____
_____
_____
_____
_____
_____
_____

Date: _____

My Bible verse of the day:
_____
_____
_____
_____
_____
_____

What this verse means in
my life today:
_____
_____
_____
_____
_____
_____
_____
_____
_____
_____

My prayer to God:
_____
_____
_____
_____
_____
_____
_____
_____
_____
_____

Date: _____

Today my heart is full of:

_____
_____
_____
_____
_____
_____

I hear God reminding me:

_____
_____
_____
_____
_____
_____
_____
_____
_____

I believe God is teaching me:

_____
_____
_____
_____
_____
_____
_____
_____
_____

Date: _____

My Bible verse of the day:

_____
_____
_____
_____
_____
_____

What this verse means in
my life today:

_____
_____
_____
_____
_____
_____
_____
_____
_____
_____
_____

My prayer to God:

_____
_____
_____
_____
_____
_____
_____
_____
_____
_____
_____

Date: _____

Today I feel blessed because:

_____
_____
_____
_____
_____
_____

I feel God in my heart when I:

_____
_____
_____
_____
_____
_____
_____
_____
_____

I have faith that God will:

_____
_____
_____
_____
_____
_____
_____
_____
_____

Date: _____

My Bible verse of the day:

_____
_____
_____
_____
_____

*What this verse means in
my life today:*

_____
_____
_____
_____
_____
_____
_____
_____
_____
_____

My prayer to God:

_____
_____
_____
_____
_____
_____
_____
_____

Date: _____

My Bible verse of the day:

_____
_____
_____
_____
_____
_____

What this verse means in my life today:

_____
_____
_____
_____
_____
_____
_____
_____
_____

My prayer to God:

_____
_____
_____
_____
_____
_____
_____
_____
_____
_____

Date: _____

Deep in my heart I feel:

_____
_____
_____
_____
_____
_____

I thank God for:

_____
_____
_____
_____
_____
_____
_____
_____
_____

Today I can serve God by:

_____
_____
_____
_____
_____
_____
_____
_____
_____
_____

Date: _____

My Bible verse of the day:

_____
_____
_____
_____
_____
_____

What this verse means in my life today:

_____
_____
_____
_____
_____
_____
_____
_____

My prayer to God:

_____
_____
_____
_____
_____
_____
_____
_____
_____
_____
_____

Date: _____

Today my heart is full of:

_____
_____
_____
_____
_____

I hear God reminding me:

_____
_____
_____
_____

_____
_____
_____
_____
_____
_____

I believe God is teaching me:

_____
_____
_____
_____
_____
_____
_____
_____
_____
_____
_____

Date: _____

My Bible verse of the day:

_____
_____
_____
_____
_____
_____

What this verse means in my life today:

_____
_____
_____
_____
_____
_____
_____
_____
_____

My prayer to God:

_____
_____
_____
_____
_____
_____
_____
_____
_____
_____
_____

Date: _____

Today I feel blessed because:

_____
_____
_____
_____
_____
_____

I feel God in my heart when I:

_____
_____
_____
_____
_____
_____
_____
_____
_____
_____

I have faith that God will:

_____
_____
_____
_____
_____
_____
_____
_____
_____
_____
_____
_____

Date: _____

My Bible verse of the day:

_____
_____
_____
_____
_____
_____
_____

What this verse means in my life today:

_____
_____
_____
_____
_____
_____
_____
_____
_____
_____

My prayer to God:

_____
_____
_____
_____
_____
_____
_____
_____
_____
_____
_____

Date:

My Bible verse of the day:

_____
_____
_____
_____
_____
_____

*What this verse means in
my life today:*

_____
_____
_____
_____
_____
_____
_____
_____
_____

My prayer to God:

_____
_____
_____
_____
_____
_____
_____
_____
_____

Date: _____

Deep in my heart I feel:

_____
_____
_____
_____
_____
_____

I thank God for:

_____
_____
_____
_____
_____
_____
_____
_____
_____

*Today I can serve
God by:*

_____
_____
_____
_____
_____
_____
_____
_____
_____

Date: _____

My Bible verse of the day:

_____
_____
_____
_____
_____
_____

*What this verse means in
my life today:*

_____
_____
_____
_____
_____
_____
_____
_____
_____
_____

My prayer to God:

_____
_____
_____
_____
_____
_____
_____
_____
_____
_____

Date: _____

Today my heart is full of:

_____
_____
_____
_____
_____
_____

I hear God reminding me:

_____
_____
_____
_____
_____
_____
_____
_____
_____

I believe God is teaching me:

_____
_____
_____
_____
_____
_____
_____
_____
_____
_____
_____
_____

Date: _____

My Bible verse of the day:

_____
_____
_____
_____
_____
_____
_____

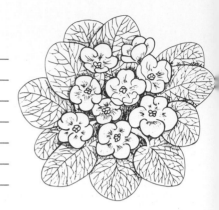

What this verse means in my life today:

_____
_____
_____
_____
_____
_____
_____
_____
_____
_____

My prayer to God:

_____
_____
_____
_____
_____
_____
_____
_____
_____
_____
_____
_____

Date: _____

Today I feel blessed because:

_____
_____
_____
_____
_____
_____

I feel God in my heart when I:

_____
_____
_____
_____
_____
_____
_____
_____
_____

I have faith that God will:

_____
_____
_____
_____
_____
_____
_____
_____
_____
_____

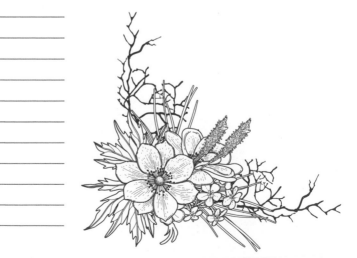

Date: _____

My Bible verse of the day:
_____
_____
_____
_____
_____
_____

What this verse means in
my life today:
_____
_____
_____
_____
_____
_____
_____
_____
_____
_____

My prayer to God:
_____
_____
_____
_____
_____
_____
_____
_____
_____
_____

Date: _____

My Bible verse of the day:

_____
_____
_____
_____
_____
_____

What this verse means in my life today:

_____
_____
_____
_____
_____
_____
_____
_____
_____

My prayer to God:

_____
_____
_____
_____
_____
_____
_____
_____
_____
_____

Date: _____

Deep in my heart I feel:

_____
_____
_____
_____
_____
_____

I thank God for:

_____
_____
_____
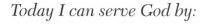
_____
_____
_____
_____
_____
_____
_____
_____

Today I can serve God by:

_____
_____
_____
_____
_____
_____
_____
_____
_____
_____
_____
_____

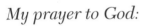

Date: _____

My Bible verse of the day:

_____
_____
_____
_____
_____
_____

What this verse means in my life today:

_____
_____
_____
_____
_____
_____
_____
_____
_____

My prayer to God:

_____
_____
_____
_____
_____
_____
_____
_____
_____
_____

Date: _____

Today my heart is full of:

_____
_____
_____
_____
_____
_____

I hear God reminding me:

_____
_____
_____
_____
_____
_____
_____
_____
_____
_____
_____

I believe God is teaching me:

_____
_____
_____
_____
_____
_____
_____
_____
_____
_____
_____

Date: _____

My Bible verse of the day:

_____
_____
_____
_____
_____
_____

What this verse means in my life today:

_____
_____
_____
_____
_____
_____
_____
_____
_____

My prayer to God:

_____
_____
_____
_____
_____
_____
_____
_____
_____
_____
_____
_____

Date: _____

Today I feel blessed because:

_____
_____
_____
_____
_____
_____

I feel God in my heart when I:

_____
_____
_____
_____
_____
_____
_____
_____
_____
_____

I have faith that God will:

_____
_____
_____
_____
_____
_____
_____
_____
_____
_____
_____
_____

Date: _____

My Bible verse of the day:

_____
_____
_____
_____
_____
_____

What this verse means in my life today:

_____
_____
_____
_____
_____
_____
_____
_____
_____
_____

My prayer to God:

_____
_____
_____
_____
_____
_____
_____
_____
_____

Date: _____

My Bible verse of the day:
_____
_____
_____
_____
_____
_____

What this verse means in
my life today:
_____
_____
_____
_____
_____
_____
_____
_____
_____
_____
_____

My prayer to God:
_____
_____
_____
_____
_____
_____
_____
_____
_____
_____
_____

Date: _____

Deep in my heart I feel:

_____
_____
_____
_____
_____
_____

I thank God for:

_____
_____
_____
_____
_____
_____
_____
_____
_____
_____

Today I can serve God by:

_____
_____
_____
_____
_____
_____
_____
_____
_____
_____
_____

Date: _____

My Bible verse of the day:

_____
_____
_____
_____
_____
_____

What this verse means in
my life today:

_____
_____
_____
_____
_____
_____
_____
_____
_____
_____
_____

My prayer to God:

_____
_____
_____
_____
_____
_____
_____
_____
_____
_____

Date: _____

Today my heart is full of:

_____
_____
_____
_____
_____
_____

I hear God reminding me:

_____
_____
_____
_____
_____
_____
_____
_____
_____
_____

I believe God is teaching me:

_____
_____
_____
_____
_____
_____
_____
_____
_____
_____
_____

Date: _____

My Bible verse of the day:

_____
_____
_____
_____
_____
_____

What this verse means in my life today:

_____
_____
_____
_____
_____
_____
_____
_____
_____
_____

My prayer to God:

_____
_____
_____
_____
_____
_____
_____
_____
_____
_____
_____
_____

Date: _____

Today I feel blessed because:

_____
_____
_____
_____
_____
_____
_____

I feel God in my heart when I:

_____
_____
_____
_____
_____
_____
_____
_____
_____
_____

I have faith that God will:

_____
_____
_____
_____
_____
_____
_____
_____
_____
_____
_____
_____

Date: _____

My Bible verse of the day:

_____
_____
_____
_____
_____
_____

*What this verse means in
my life today:*

_____
_____
_____
_____
_____
_____
_____
_____
_____
_____

My prayer to God:

_____
_____
_____
_____
_____
_____
_____
_____
_____
_____

Date: _____

My Bible verse of the day:

_____
_____
_____
_____
_____
_____

What this verse means in my life today:

_____
_____
_____
_____
_____
_____
_____
_____
_____

My prayer to God:

_____
_____
_____
_____
_____
_____
_____
_____
_____

Date: _____

Deep in my heart I feel:

_____
_____
_____
_____
_____

I thank God for:

_____
_____
_____
_____
_____
_____
_____
_____
_____
_____

Today I can serve God by:

_____
_____
_____
_____
_____
_____
_____
_____
_____
_____
_____

Date: _____

My Bible verse of the day:

_____
_____
_____
_____
_____
_____

What this verse means in my life today:

_____
_____
_____
_____
_____
_____
_____
_____
_____

My prayer to God:

_____
_____
_____
_____
_____
_____
_____
_____
_____
_____
_____

Date: _____

Today my heart is full of:

_____
_____
_____
_____
_____
_____
_____

I hear God reminding me:

_____
_____
_____
_____
_____
_____
_____
_____
_____
_____

I believe God is teaching me:

_____
_____
_____
_____
_____
_____
_____
_____
_____
_____

Date: _____

My Bible verse of the day:

_____
_____
_____
_____
_____
_____
_____

What this verse means in my life today:

_____
_____
_____
_____
_____
_____
_____
_____
_____
_____

My prayer to God:

_____
_____
_____
_____
_____
_____
_____
_____
_____

Date: _____

Today I feel blessed because:

_____
_____
_____
_____
_____

I feel God in my heart when I:

_____
_____

_____
_____
_____
_____
_____
_____
_____
_____

I have faith that God will:

_____
_____
_____
_____
_____
_____
_____
_____
_____
_____
_____
_____

Date: _____

My Bible verse of the day:

_____
_____
_____
_____
_____
_____

What this verse means in my life today:

_____
_____
_____
_____
_____
_____
_____
_____
_____
_____

My prayer to God:

_____
_____
_____
_____
_____
_____
_____
_____
_____
_____
_____
_____
_____

Date: _____

My Bible verse of the day:

_____
_____
_____
_____
_____
_____

What this verse means in my life today:

_____
_____
_____
_____
_____
_____
_____
_____
_____
_____

My prayer to God:

_____
_____
_____
_____
_____
_____
_____
_____
_____
_____
_____

Date: _____

Deep in my heart I feel:

_____
_____
_____
_____
_____
_____

I thank God for:

_____
_____
_____
_____
_____
_____
_____
_____

Today I can serve God by:

_____
_____
_____
_____
_____
_____
_____
_____
_____

Date: _____

My Bible verse of the day:

_____
_____
_____
_____
_____
_____

What this verse means in my life today:

_____
_____
_____
_____
_____
_____
_____
_____
_____
_____
_____

My prayer to God:

_____
_____
_____
_____
_____
_____
_____
_____
_____
_____
_____

Date: _____

Today my heart is full of:

_____
_____
_____
_____
_____
_____

I hear God reminding me:

_____
_____
_____
_____
_____
_____
_____
_____
_____

I believe God is teaching me:

_____
_____
_____
_____
_____
_____
_____
_____
_____
_____
_____

Date: _____

My Bible verse of the day:

_____
_____
_____
_____
_____
_____

What this verse means in my life today:

_____
_____
_____
_____
_____
_____
_____
_____
_____
_____
_____

My prayer to God:

_____
_____
_____
_____
_____
_____
_____
_____
_____
_____
_____
_____

Date: _____

Today I feel blessed because:

_____
_____
_____
_____
_____
_____
_____

I feel God in my heart when I:

_____
_____
_____
_____
_____
_____
_____
_____
_____
_____

I have faith that
God will:

_____
_____
_____
_____
_____
_____
_____
_____
_____

Date: _____

My Bible verse of the day:

_____
_____
_____
_____
_____
_____

What this verse means in my life today:

_____
_____
_____
_____
_____
_____
_____
_____
_____
_____
_____

My prayer to God:

_____
_____
_____
_____
_____
_____
_____
_____
_____
_____
_____

Date: _____

My Bible verse of the day:

_____
_____
_____
_____
_____
_____

What this verse means in my life today:

_____
_____
_____
_____
_____
_____
_____
_____
_____
_____

My prayer to God:

_____
_____
_____
_____
_____
_____
_____
_____
_____
_____
_____

Date: _____

Deep in my heart I feel:

_____
_____
_____
_____
_____
_____

I thank God for:

_____
_____
_____
_____
_____
_____
_____
_____
_____
_____

Today I can serve God by:

_____
_____
_____
_____
_____
_____
_____
_____
_____
_____
_____

Date: _____

My Bible verse of the day:

_____
_____
_____
_____
_____
_____

What this verse means in my life today:

_____
_____
_____
_____
_____
_____
_____
_____
_____

My prayer to God:

_____
_____
_____
_____
_____
_____
_____
_____
_____
_____
_____

Date: _____

Today my heart is full of:

_____
_____
_____
_____
_____
_____

I hear God reminding me:

_____
_____
_____
_____
_____
_____
_____
_____
_____
_____
_____

I believe God is teaching me:

_____
_____
_____
_____
_____
_____
_____
_____
_____
_____
_____
_____
_____
_____

Date: _____

My Bible verse of the day:

_____
_____
_____
_____
_____
_____

What this verse means in my life today:

_____
_____
_____
_____
_____
_____
_____
_____
_____

My prayer to God:

_____
_____
_____
_____
_____
_____
_____
_____
_____
_____
_____

Date: _____

Today I feel blessed because:

_____
_____
_____
_____
_____
_____

I feel God in my heart when I:

_____
_____
_____
_____
_____
_____
_____
_____
_____
_____
_____

I have faith that God will:

_____
_____
_____
_____
_____
_____
_____
_____
_____
_____
_____
_____

Date: _____

My Bible verse of the day:

_____
_____
_____
_____
_____
_____

What this verse means in my life today:

_____
_____
_____
_____
_____
_____
_____
_____
_____

My prayer to God:

_____
_____
_____
_____
_____
_____
_____
_____
_____

Date: _____

My Bible verse of the day:

_____
_____
_____
_____
_____
_____

What this verse means in my life today:

_____
_____
_____
_____
_____
_____
_____
_____
_____
_____
_____
_____

My prayer to God:

_____
_____
_____
_____
_____
_____
_____
_____
_____
_____
_____
_____

Date: _____

Deep in my heart I feel:

_____
_____
_____
_____
_____
_____
_____

I thank God for:

_____
_____
_____
_____
_____
_____
_____
_____
_____
_____

Today I can serve God by:

_____
_____
_____
_____
_____
_____
_____
_____
_____
_____
_____
_____

Date: _____

My Bible verse of the day:

_____
_____
_____
_____
_____
_____

What this verse means in my life today:

_____
_____
_____
_____
_____
_____
_____
_____
_____
_____

My prayer to God:

_____
_____
_____
_____
_____
_____
_____
_____
_____
_____

Date: _____

Today my heart is full of:

_____
_____
_____
_____
_____
_____

I hear God reminding me:

_____
_____
_____
_____
_____
_____
_____
_____
_____

I believe God is teaching me:

_____
_____
_____
_____
_____
_____
_____
_____
_____
_____

Date: _____

My Bible verse of the day:

_____
_____
_____
_____
_____
_____

What this verse means in
my life today:

_____
_____
_____
_____
_____
_____
_____
_____
_____
_____
_____

My prayer to God:

_____
_____
_____
_____
_____
_____
_____
_____
_____
_____
_____
_____

Date: _____

Today I feel blessed because:

_____
_____
_____
_____
_____
_____

I feel God in my heart when I:

_____
_____
_____
_____
_____
_____
_____
_____
_____
_____

I have faith that God will:

_____
_____
_____
_____
_____
_____
_____
_____
_____
_____
_____
_____

Date: _____

My Bible verse of the day:

_____
_____
_____
_____
_____

What this verse means in
my life today:

_____
_____
_____
_____
_____
_____
_____
_____
_____
_____

My prayer to God:

_____
_____
_____
_____
_____
_____
_____
_____
_____

Date: _____

My Bible verse of the day:

_____
_____
_____
_____
_____
_____

What this verse means in my life today:

_____
_____
_____
_____
_____
_____
_____
_____
_____

My prayer to God:

_____
_____
_____
_____
_____
_____
_____
_____
_____

Date: _____

Deep in my heart I feel:

_____
_____
_____
_____
_____
_____

I thank God for:

_____
_____
_____
_____
_____
_____
_____
_____
_____
_____

Today I can serve God by:

_____
_____
_____
_____
_____
_____
_____
_____
_____
_____
_____

Date: _____

My Bible verse of the day:

_____
_____
_____
_____
_____
_____

What this verse means in my life today:

_____
_____
_____
_____
_____
_____
_____
_____
_____

My prayer to God:

_____
_____
_____
_____
_____
_____
_____
_____
_____
_____
_____
_____

Date: _____

Today my heart is full of:

_____
_____
_____
_____
_____
_____

I hear God reminding me:

_____
_____
_____
_____

_____
_____
_____
_____
_____
_____
_____

I believe God is teaching me:

_____
_____
_____
_____
_____
_____
_____
_____
_____
_____
_____
_____
_____

Date: _____

My Bible verse of the day:

_____
_____
_____
_____
_____
_____

What this verse means in my life today:

_____
_____
_____
_____
_____
_____
_____
_____
_____

My prayer to God:

_____
_____
_____
_____
_____
_____
_____
_____
_____

Date: _____

Today I feel blessed because:

_____
_____
_____
_____
_____
_____

I feel God in my heart when I:

_____
_____

_____
_____
_____
_____
_____
_____
_____
_____
_____

I have faith that God will:

_____
_____
_____
_____
_____
_____
_____
_____
_____
_____
_____
_____
_____
_____

Date: _____

My Bible verse of the day:

_____
_____
_____
_____
_____
_____

What this verse means in my life today:

_____
_____
_____
_____
_____
_____
_____
_____
_____

My prayer to God:

_____
_____
_____

_____
_____
_____
_____
_____
_____
_____
_____

Date: _____

My Bible verse of the day:

_____
_____
_____
_____
_____

What this verse means in my life today:

_____
_____
_____
_____
_____
_____
_____
_____
_____
_____
_____

My prayer to God:

_____
_____
_____
_____
_____
_____
_____
_____
_____
_____
_____

Date: _____

Deep in my heart I feel:

_____
_____
_____
_____
_____
_____

I thank God for:

_____
_____
_____
_____
_____
_____
_____
_____
_____
_____

Today I can serve God by:

_____
_____
_____
_____
_____
_____
_____
_____
_____

Date: _____

My Bible verse of the day:

_____
_____
_____
_____
_____
_____

What this verse means in
my life today:

_____
_____
_____
_____
_____
_____
_____
_____
_____
_____

My prayer to God:

_____
_____
_____
_____
_____
_____
_____
_____
_____
_____
_____

Date: _____

Today my heart is full of:

_____
_____
_____
_____
_____
_____

I hear God reminding me:

_____
_____
_____
_____
_____
_____
_____
_____
_____

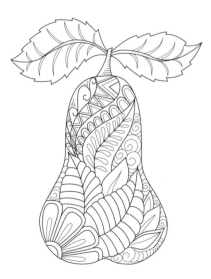

I believe God is teaching me:

_____
_____
_____
_____
_____
_____
_____
_____
_____
_____
_____

Date: _____

My Bible verse of the day:

_____
_____
_____
_____
_____
_____

What this verse means in my life today:

_____
_____
_____
_____
_____
_____
_____
_____
_____
_____
_____

My prayer to God:

_____
_____
_____
_____
_____
_____
_____
_____
_____
_____
_____
_____

Date: _____

Today I feel blessed because:

_____
_____
_____
_____
_____
_____

I feel God in my heart when I:

_____
_____
_____
_____
_____
_____
_____
_____

I have faith that
God will:

_____
_____
_____
_____
_____
_____
_____
_____
_____

Date: _____

My Bible verse of the day:
_____
_____
_____
_____
_____
_____

What this verse means in
my life today:
_____
_____
_____
_____
_____
_____
_____
_____
_____
_____

My prayer to God:
_____
_____
_____
_____
_____
_____
_____
_____
_____
_____

Date: _____

My Bible verse of the day:

_____
_____
_____
_____
_____
_____

What this verse means in my life today:

_____
_____
_____
_____
_____
_____
_____
_____
_____
_____

My prayer to God:

_____
_____
_____
_____
_____
_____
_____
_____
_____
_____
_____
_____

Date: _____

Deep in my heart I feel:

_____
_____
_____
_____
_____
_____

I thank God for:

_____
_____
_____
_____
_____
_____
_____
_____
_____
_____

Today I can serve God by:

_____
_____
_____
_____
_____
_____
_____
_____
_____
_____

Date: _____

My Bible verse of the day:

_____
_____
_____
_____
_____
_____

What this verse means in my life today:

_____
_____
_____
_____
_____
_____
_____
_____
_____

My prayer to God:

_____
_____
_____
_____
_____
_____
_____
_____
_____
_____

Date: _____

Today my heart is full of:

_____
_____
_____
_____
_____
_____

I hear God reminding me:

_____
_____
_____
_____
_____
_____
_____
_____
_____
_____

I believe God is teaching me:

_____
_____
_____
_____
_____
_____
_____
_____
_____
_____
_____

Date: _____

My Bible verse of the day:

_____
_____
_____
_____
_____
_____

What this verse means in my life today:

_____
_____
_____
_____
_____
_____
_____
_____
_____

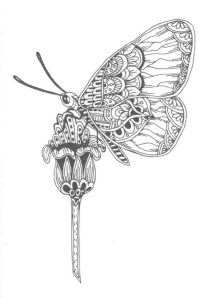

My prayer to God:

_____
_____
_____
_____
_____
_____
_____
_____
_____
_____
_____

Date: _____

Today I feel blessed because:

_____
_____
_____
_____
_____

I feel God in my heart when I:

_____
_____
_____
_____
_____
_____
_____
_____
_____
_____
_____

I have faith that God will:

_____
_____
_____
_____
_____
_____
_____
_____
_____
_____
_____

Date: _____

My Bible verse of the day:

_____
_____
_____
_____
_____
_____

What this verse means in my life today:

_____
_____
_____
_____
_____
_____
_____
_____
_____
_____

My prayer to God:

_____
_____
_____
_____
_____
_____
_____
_____
_____
_____
_____

Date: _____

My Bible verse of the day:

_____
_____
_____
_____
_____
_____

*What this verse means in
my life today:*

_____
_____
_____

_____
_____
_____
_____
_____
_____
_____

My prayer to God:

_____
_____
_____
_____
_____
_____
_____
_____
_____
_____

Date: _____

Deep in my heart I feel:

_____
_____
_____
_____
_____
_____

I thank God for:

_____
_____
_____
_____
_____
_____
_____
_____
_____

Today I can serve God by:

_____
_____
_____
_____
_____
_____
_____
_____
_____

Date: _____

My Bible verse of the day:

_____
_____
_____
_____
_____
_____

What this verse means in
my life today:

_____
_____
_____
_____
_____
_____
_____
_____
_____
_____
_____
_____

My prayer to God:

_____
_____
_____
_____
_____
_____
_____
_____
_____
_____

Date: _____

Today my heart is full of:

_____
_____
_____
_____
_____
_____

I hear God reminding me:

_____
_____
_____
_____
_____
_____
_____
_____
_____

I believe God is
teaching me:

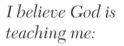

_____
_____
_____
_____
_____
_____
_____
_____
_____
_____

Date: _____

My Bible verse of the day:

_____
_____
_____
_____
_____
_____

*What this verse means in
my life today:*

_____
_____
_____
_____
_____
_____
_____
_____
_____
_____
_____

My prayer to God:

_____
_____
_____
_____
_____
_____
_____
_____
_____
_____

Date: _____

Today I feel blessed because:

_____
_____
_____
_____
_____
_____

I feel God in my heart when I:

_____
_____
_____
_____
_____
_____
_____
_____
_____

I have faith that God will:

_____
_____
_____
_____
_____
_____
_____
_____
_____
_____
_____

Date: _____

My Bible verse of the day:

_____
_____
_____
_____
_____
_____

*What this verse means in
my life today:*

_____
_____
_____
_____
_____
_____
_____
_____
_____
_____
_____

My prayer to God:

_____
_____
_____
_____
_____
_____
_____
_____
_____
_____

Date: _____

My Bible verse of the day:

_____
_____
_____
_____
_____
_____

What this verse means in my life today:

_____
_____
_____
_____
_____
_____
_____
_____
_____
_____

My prayer to God:

_____
_____
_____
_____
_____
_____
_____
_____
_____
_____

Date: _____

Deep in my heart I feel:

_____
_____
_____
_____
_____

I thank God for:

_____
_____
_____
_____
_____
_____
_____
_____
_____

Today I can serve God by:

_____
_____
_____
_____
_____
_____
_____
_____
_____

Date: _____

My Bible verse of the day:

_____
_____
_____
_____
_____
_____

What this verse means in my life today:

_____
_____
_____
_____
_____
_____
_____
_____
_____
_____

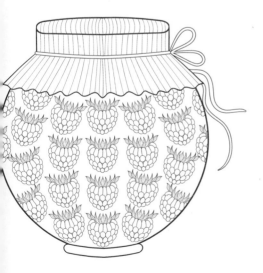

My prayer to God:

_____
_____
_____
_____
_____
_____
_____
_____
_____
_____

Date: _____

Today my heart is full of:

_____
_____
_____
_____
_____
_____

I hear God reminding me:

_____
_____
_____
_____
_____
_____
_____
_____
_____
_____

I believe God is teaching me:

_____
_____
_____
_____
_____
_____
_____
_____
_____
_____

Date: _____

My Bible verse of the day:

_____

_____

_____

_____

_____

_____

What this verse means in my life today:

_____

_____

_____

_____

_____

_____

_____

_____

My prayer to God:

_____

_____

_____

_____

_____

_____

_____

_____

_____

_____

Date: _____

Today I feel blessed because:

_____
_____
_____
_____
_____

I feel God in my heart when I:

_____
_____

_____
_____
_____
_____
_____
_____
_____
_____

I have faith that God will:

_____
_____
_____
_____
_____
_____
_____
_____
_____
_____
_____
_____

Date: _____

My Bible verse of the day:

_____
_____
_____
_____
_____
_____
_____

What this verse means in my life today:

_____
_____
_____
_____
_____
_____
_____
_____
_____
_____

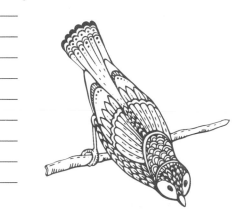

My prayer to God:

_____
_____
_____
_____
_____
_____
_____
_____
_____